KINGSHA

919.8

EYEWITNESS ⟨◉⟩ GUIDES

ARCTIC &
ANTARCTIC

Arctic plant

Reindeer skin winter coat from Siberia

Net for catching ptarmigan

Siberian shaman's staff

Antarctic explorer's compass

Siberian ivory model of reindeer drawing a sledge

Rosebay
willow
herb

Snowshoe
for a pony

EYEWITNESS  GUIDES

ARCTIC &
ANTARCTIC

Written by
BARBARA TAYLOR

Photographed by
GEOFF BRIGHTLING

Carving of polar
bear from Canada

DK

DORLING KINDERSLEY
London • New York • Stuttgart

Model of Greenland canoe

Engraved ivory

Cribbage board
made from
walrus tusk

DK

A DORLING KINDERSLEY BOOK

Project editor Gillian Denton
Art editor Jane Tetzlaff
Managing editor Simon Adams
Managing art editor Julia Harris
Researcher Céline Carez
Editorial Assistance Djinn von Noorden, David Pickering
Production Catherine Semark
Picture research Clive Webster

This Eyewitness ® Guide has been conceived by
Dorling Kindersley Limited and Editions Gallimard

First published in Great Britain in 1995
by Dorling Kindersley Limited,
9 Henrietta Street, London WC2E 8PS

4 6 8 10 9 7 5

Copyright © 1995 Dorling Kindersley Limited, London

Visit us on the World Wide Web at
http://www.dk.com

All rights reserved. No part of this publication may be
reproduced, stored in a retrieval system, or transmitted
in any form or by any means, electronic, mechanical,
photocopying, recording or otherwise, without the
prior written permission of the copyright owner.

A CIP catalogue record for this book is
available from the British Library.

ISBN 0 7513 6033 3

Filmsetting by Litho Link Ltd,
Welshpool, Powys

Colour reproduction by
Colourscan, Singapore
Printed in Singapore by Toppan

Shaman's
eagle from
Siberia

Siberian shaman's apron

Both the Arctic and
Antarctic support
some plant life

Husky dogs

Contents

Snowy owl

The ends of the earth

THE TWO POLAR REGIONS at the very ends of the earth are among the coldest, windiest, and most remote places on the planet. A huge, frozen ocean – the Arctic – surrounds the North Pole, while a vast area of frozen land – Antarctica – surrounds the South Pole. Both the Arctic and Antarctic have long, dark, freezing winters. During the short summer days, the sun shines all the time, and animals flock to these areas to feed and nest. The Arctic and Antarctic are the last two wilderness areas on earth, although the Arctic has already been exploited for its mineral wealth, and both polar regions are increasingly threatened by pollution, mining, and other human pressures.

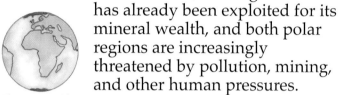

The position of the Arctic and Antarctic

TRAPPED BY THE ICE
In 1596, a Dutch explorer, William Barents, set off on his third attempt to find a route from Europe to China and India around the North Pole. When his ship was trapped by sea ice, he and his crew were forced to winter ashore, building a cabin from the wrecked ship. In spring, the men set off for Europe in the ship's boats. Barents himself died, but his men survived.

Long tongues of ice extend into the sea from the edges of ice sheets

An unstructured slush known as frazil ice forms below the surface

MYSTERY LAND

In the fourth century BC, the Greek philosopher Aristotle suggested the existence of a southern landmass, known as *Terra australis incognita* – the unknown continent. Map-makers included a huge southern continent on their maps until 1773, but it was not until the mid-18th century that people saw Antarctica for the first time when James Cook went to find out what was really there.

NORTHERN LIGHTS
Auroras are wispy curtains of light which appear in the sky above the poles. They can sometimes take the form of brilliantly coloured shooting rays. Auroras are caused by charged particles from the sun striking gases in the earth's atmosphere above the poles. This makes the gases give off light.

MIDNIGHT SUN
In regions near the North and South poles the sun never sets for several months during the summer. This happens because of the tilt of the earth towards the sun. While one pole has constant daylight the other is shrouded in winter darkness because the sun never rises.

In quiet waters ice often begins as thin plates, known as grease ice because they coat the water with an oily sheen

Freezing builds the ice into thicker layers; wind and waves work to break it up

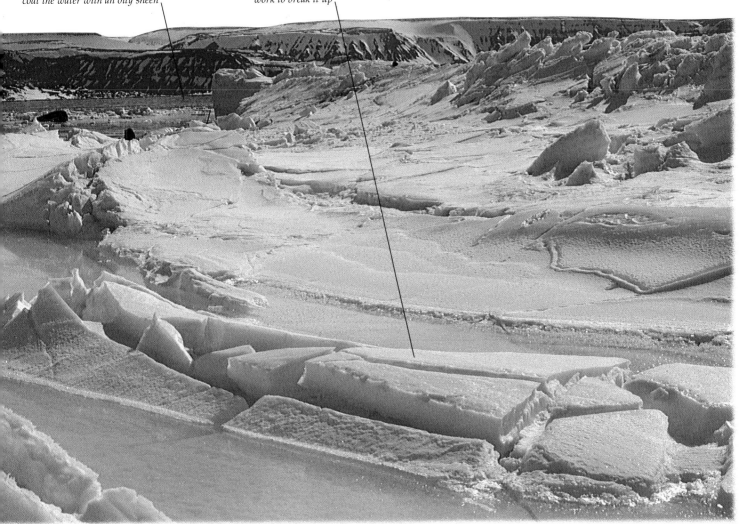

The Arctic and tundra

At the centre of the Arctic region is a vast area of permanently frozen ice floating on the Arctic Ocean. The Arctic region also includes the largest island in the world, Greenland, the island of Spitsbergen, and the northern edges of North America, Asia, and Europe. The ice-free land in the Arctic is called tundra, which means "treeless plain" in Russian. The landscape is low and flat, with many lichens, mosses, grasses, and sprawling, low bushes. Trees cannot grow in the true Arctic because they are unable to stand up to the intense cold and fierce winter winds. Water from the warmer Pacific and Atlantic Oceans sometimes flows into the Arctic Ocean, warming the sea and air and clearing ice from the coasts in summer.

MAPPING THE COAST
In 1819–1822 Sir John Franklin, later to lose his life searching for the elusive northwest passage (pp. 52–53), made a hazardous land expedition charting the coast of Canada. At one point he took to canoe which was particularly hazardous as the ice was breaking up. Wooden ships and boats of the 19th century could easily be crushed or trapped by ice.

Marshy pools form because permafrost prevents water from draining away

The 'tree line' where forest gives way to tundra is often taken to be the southern boundary of the true Arctic

Frozen layer, called permafrost, a little way below the surface; it never thaws out

BEAR JOURNEYS
Polar bears live only in the Arctic. They make long journeys across the Arctic pack ice, hunting for seals. The bears are expert divers and swimmers, and often hitch rides on ice floes. One polar bear was found swimming 320 km (200 miles) from land. Polar bears can also dive more than 15 m (50 ft) from the top of icebergs into the water.

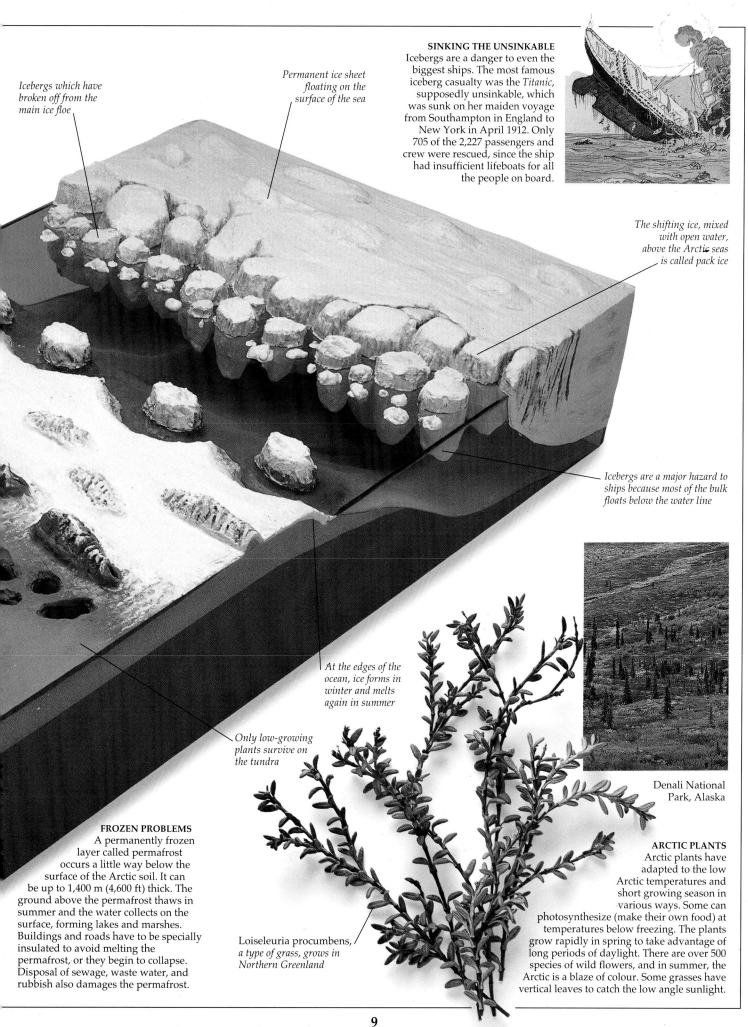

Icebergs which have
broken off from the
main ice floe

Permanent ice sheet
floating on the
surface of the sea

SINKING THE UNSINKABLE
Icebergs are a danger to even the
biggest ships. The most famous
iceberg casualty was the *Titanic*,
supposedly unsinkable, which
was sunk on her maiden voyage
from Southampton in England to
New York in April 1912. Only
705 of the 2,227 passengers and
crew were rescued, since the ship
had insufficient lifeboats for all
the people on board.

*The shifting ice, mixed
with open water,
above the Arctic seas
is called pack ice*

*Icebergs are a major hazard to
ships because most of the bulk
floats below the water line*

*At the edges of the
ocean, ice forms in
winter and melts
again in summer*

*Only low-growing
plants survive on
the tundra*

Denali National
Park, Alaska

FROZEN PROBLEMS
A permanently frozen
layer called permafrost
occurs a little way below the
surface of the Arctic soil. It can
be up to 1,400 m (4,600 ft) thick. The
ground above the permafrost thaws in
summer and the water collects on the
surface, forming lakes and marshes.
Buildings and roads have to be specially
insulated to avoid melting the
permafrost, or they begin to collapse.
Disposal of sewage, waste water, and
rubbish also damages the permafrost.

*Loiseleuria procumbens,
a type of grass, grows in
Northern Greenland*

ARCTIC PLANTS
Arctic plants have
adapted to the low
Arctic temperatures and
short growing season in
various ways. Some can
photosynthesize (make their own food) at
temperatures below freezing. The plants
grow rapidly in spring to take advantage of
long periods of daylight. There are over 500
species of wild flowers, and in summer, the
Arctic is a blaze of colour. Some grasses have
vertical leaves to catch the low angle sunlight.

The Antarctic

THE CONTINENT OF ANTARCTICA is twice the size of Australia, and one and a half times the size of the United States. It is also three times higher than any other continent on earth. The height of the land is one major reason for the extreme cold in Antarctica, where the average winter temperature is -60°C (-76°F). Antarctica's severe climate, and its isolation from other continents, has greatly reduced the variety of its wildlife – the largest animal that lives on land all year round is a tiny insect. During the summer, however, many animals including penguins, whales, and seals, visit the continent to take advantage of the plentiful food supply and safe breeding sites around the coasts. Plants are very sparse, with the flora dominated by lichens, mosses, and liverworts.

SOLE SURVIVOR
Mosses are one of the few plants able to survive in Antarctica. There are about 80 species of these tough little plants in the region, which grow in dense mats and cushions for protection from the weather. Dead moss builds up to form banks of peat which can be several metres thick.

WARMER CLIMATE
Antarctica was not always cold. Fossil ferns (above) provide evidence of a warmer, sub-tropical climate about 70 million years ago. Over hundreds of millions of years, the land that is now Antarctica probably drifted to the bottom of the world from near the equator.

SOUTH POLE PENGUINS
Penguins live only in the southern hemisphere. In the Arctic they are replaced by auks, which look like penguins and have a similar lifestyle. Auks can fly, but penguins are flightless.

Only 10 percent of an iceberg is visible above water level

ICEBERGS
Icebergs form when snow falls on the polar plateau and turns into ice. The ice is compacted, and flows down towards the coastal ice shelves where it is broken up by ocean tides, currents, and waves. This produces icebergs. Some icebergs are so large – up to 240 km (150 miles) long and 110 km (70 miles) wide – that they can be tracked by satellites for several years before they melt.

COILED CLUES
Swimming shellfish with coiled shells, called ammonites, were common in the warm seas of pre-historic times. The last ammonites died out about 65 million years ago, but fossil ammonites found on Antarctica show that Antarctic seas were warmer millions of years ago.

WEIGHT OF ICE
About 98 percent of Antarctica is covered by an immense ice sheet, which in some places is over 4 km (2.5 miles) thick. Most of the mountains, and all the lower ground is buried under ice. Only a few jagged peaks, called nunataks, stick out. The enormous weight of the ice pushes most of the rocky surface of Antarctica below sea level. The ice in the lowest layers of the ice sheet is thought to be at least 200,000 years old.

DRY VALLEYS
Hidden among the Transantarctic Mountains are vast dry valleys, which are not covered by snow or ice all year round. The valleys originally dried out because the mountains held back the ice cap. Winds rushing down the valleys suck away any moisture, forming large areas of bare rock in the middle of the continent.

CLEARING THE ICE
Special ships called ice-breakers are used to keep trade routes clear of ice during the winter. Before ice-breakers, many early polar explorers saw their fragile wooden ships crushed by the power of the ice. Ice-breakers have a specially shaped bow and a reinforced hull. They push the bow on top of the ice until the weight of the ship breaks through it.

As icebergs melt they often form fascinating shapes

The erosive forces of ocean and winds combine to carve the ice

Icebergs often look blue, possibly a reflection from the water

Life in Antarctic waters

IN CONTRAST TO THE SMALL VARIETY of animals on land, there is an incredible wealth of life in the sea around Antarctica. In shallow waters, ice scrapes against the sea bed preventing any life, but in deeper waters below the crust of ice, there is a greater variety of life in the Antarctic Ocean than in the Arctic Ocean. Corals and anemones are anchored to the seabed with some 300 varieties of sponges. Many sea creatures feed on each other or on dead plankton. The cold affects the life cycles of many inhabitants. Because food is scarce most of the year, animals function more slowly. They produce fewer, larger eggs and look after them with care. Many animals live longer than their counterparts in warmer waters. Some sponges live for several centuries.

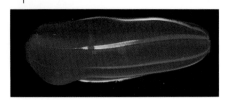

COMMON CREATURES
Antarctic squid (top) have no shell which is useful in icy waters where shells grow very slowly. They seize prey in their two long tentacles. The jellyfish (bottom) which is between 0.5 and 50 cm (0.2 in and 20 in) long is very common in Antarctic waters.

DUAL PURPOSE SPINES
Sea bed animals such as the sea urchin (*Sterechinus neumayer*) may move to shallower water during the summer when they are not in danger from ice scouring the rocks on which they live. Their dense covering of mobile spines is used both for movement and for defence.

The spines of sea urchins are often poisonous

Point at the end of the leg to dig for food in the sea bed

SEA LEGS
Orange sea spiders with ten to twelve giant legs are found in deeper Antarctic waters. The pyctogonid spider (*Decolopoda australis*) has a diameter of 15 cm (6 in). It feeds on sea anemones and, like other Antarctic sea creatures, develops very slowly.

COLD GIANTS
Many of the Antarctic's bottom-living invertebrates (creatures without backbones) are giants, such as this giant isopod *Glyptonotus antarcticus*, a relative of the woodlouse. It fills the ecological niche occupied by crabs in other parts of the world, which are not present here. *Glyptonotus* grows up to 20 cm (8 in), about three times bigger than similar species elsewhere. Because growth is slow in the cold waters, slow-growing invertebrates reach larger sizes than faster-growing ones. *Glyptonotus* eats anything and scavenges around the sea bed.

As well as the main legs, the spider has several small ones

Tentacles of coral filter out small zooplankton drifting past

ON THE ROCKS
A rock face about 8–10 m (26–33 ft) below the surface of the water provides a good anchorage for sponges, bryozoans (sea mosses), and the long, hanging stalks of the soft coral *Ascolepis*. Sponges and some corals are abundant at depths of up to 1 km (0.6 mile).

Tentacles contain stinging cells which paralyze prey

TERRIBLE TENTACLES
Sea anemones capture prey such as small fish or starfish in their tentacles. The tentacles then pass the prey into the central mouth opening, ready to be digested and absorbed into the body. Waste is excreted through the mouth.

STAR TURN
The seabed around Antarctica is sometimes covered with colourful red starfish. Prey are located by smell, and grasped by rows of tube feet on the underside of the legs. Antarctic starfish live many years – one is known to have lived to the age of 39.

Tube feet for walking, digging, and grasping prey

Migrants and residents

Migratory animals follow the sun

THE NUMBER AND VARIETY of animals living near the poles changes dramatically with the seasons. Thousands of birds and mammals only visit the Arctic or Antarctic during the brief, light summer months, when it is warm and there is plenty of food available day and night. Apart from the food supply, the other advantages for summer migrants are safe places to rear their young, with few predators, and a lack of competition for food and nesting places. Often, the same traditional migration routes are used each year, but the animals also navigate using the positions of the sun, moon, and stars, the earth's magnetic field, and familiar landmarks. Journeys are often very dangerous, and many animals are killed by bad weather, lack of food, and predators before reaching their destination.

Dense down feathers help to keep the geese warm

The birds save energy by flying in a V-formation in the slipstream of the one in front

Arctic tern
Sterna paradisaea

Thick skull and solid horny band protect the brain during conflict

Musk ox
Ovibos moschatus

Powerful wings allow the tern to cover up to 40,000 km (25,000 miles) on each round trip

CHAMPION TRAVELLER
The graceful Arctic tern may see more daylight each year than any other creature. It breeds in large colonies during the Arctic summer. Then it flies all the way to the Antarctic to take advantage of the almost constant daylight and rich food supply of the Antarctic summer.

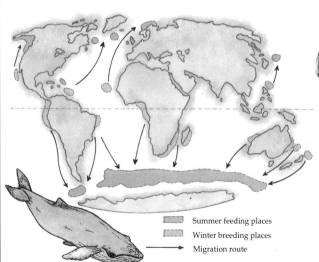

- Summer feeding places
- Winter breeding places
- Migration route

Very long outer fur retains body warmth and keeps animal dry

FOOD IN THE FREEZER
Whales in both the northern and the southern hemispheres travel to cold polar waters in summer to take advantage of the rich food supply of plankton and fish. In winter, when the sea freezes over, they migrate back to warmer tropical waters again, to breed. They eat little during their tropical stopover, relying on their immense stores of body fat built up during the summer.

MIGHTY MUSK OX
Tough, hardy musk oxen roam over the harsh tundra in herds made up of females and young, led by one or more strong bulls. In summer, herds number about ten animals, but in winter, musk oxen move south, in herds of 50 or more wherever they can find food under the snow. Their name comes from the smell given off by the males during the breeding season.

The male's antlers are larger and thicker than those of the females

Caribou
Rangifer tarandus

Caribou can move over soft ground or snow without sinking deeply

FLIGHT OF THE SNOW GEESE
Many thousands of pairs of snow geese nest in the Arctic tundra in the summer. They migrate all the way from the Gulf of Mexico, a journey of about 3,200 km (2,000 miles). On their journey, they fly in flocks of tens of thousands of birds. The shorter days at the end of summer tell the snow geese it is time to fly south once more.

SUMMER HOLIDAYS
Caribou herds are always on the move, wandering between their winter and summer feeding grounds and snatching bites of food wherever they can find it. In spring, immense herds trek northwards to feed on lichens and other low-growing tundra plants. They use well-marked trails which are often centuries old. As winter closes in, the caribou move south once more to the shelter of the forests.

Feet are tucked back during flight to make a more streamlined shape

Snow goose
Anser caerulescens

Spectacular curved horns for defence against enemies such as wolves

Dense woolly underfur and thick layers of fat under the skin keep the musk ox warm

Short, very strong legs support the massive body

Edges of hooves are sharp enough to dig through thick snow and ice to reach mosses, lichens, and roots underneath

Adaptable animals

To survive the contrasting seasons, animals have to change too. As winter approaches, some mammals grow thick fur coats, which may be white for camouflage against the snow. They store a thick layer of fat in their skin to trap extra warmth and act as a food store in lean times. Birds also have layers of fat and dense, fluffy feathers to keep out the cold. For many birds and mammals, the severe winter weather is just too much to cope with. They migrate south to warmer places, returning again in spring. Insects rest in the warmer soil over the winter, usually in the form of larvae, and are able to withstand the freezing temperatures. As summer arrives, birds and mammals moult their thick coats. Animals that turn white in winter, turn brown for summer camouflage.

FINE FURS
People in cold countries always wore fur clothes to keep warm through the coldest winters. They usually obtained them by snaring their original owners in traps.

Arctic fox
Alopex lagopus

DRESSED FOR SUMMER
In summer, the Arctic fox grows a thinner coat of brownish-grey fur over most of its body. These colours match the brownish-grey rocks of the tundra landscape, making the fox hard to see, so that it can creep up on its prey, such as lemmings, without being spotted. The fox stores food under rocks during the summer and comes back to eat it in the winter months when food is hard to find. Arctic foxes have a varied diet, eating anything from berries, shells, and dead animals to garbage, birds, and eggs. But lemmings are vital and Arctic foxes endure many weeks of starvation if there are few lemmings about.

The chest and belly are usually a pale grey-white colour

Short legs lose less heat than long ones as there is less surface area exposed to the air

Thick, bushy tail can be curled around the body for warmth during blizzards or when resting or sleeping

Antarctic ice fish
Chaenocephalus aceratus

ANTI-FREEZE IN ITS VEINS
Many Antarctic fishes have anti-freeze molecules in their bodies which enable them to live in a "supercooled" state; their body fluids remain liquid at temperatures below the point at which ice forms. Antarctic ice fish (such as the fish on the left) have almost translucent blood.

Hair under paws stops fox sinking in snow; the fox's Latin name is Alopex lagopus. Lagopus *means "hairy foot"*

Sharp claws to dig through the snow to find food

A BIRD FOR ALL SEASONS
Ptarmigans change their plumage twice a year, so that they are well camouflaged at all times. They also increase their feather density in winter. When resting overnight they sometimes burrow in snow to reduce heat loss.

Rock ptarmigan
Lagopus mutus

Dense fur coat with long hairs traps body warmth

Ears are furry inside and out for extra warmth

FINE TO BE FAT
Whales and seals are kept warm by a layer of thick fat called blubber. This fat walrus is in no danger of getting cold. Walruses can weigh up to 1,600 kg (1.6 tons), with tusks 1 m (3 ft) long.

Small, round ears and a short muzzle cut down on heat loss; foxes from warmer places have larger ears and a longer muzzle

Sharp, pointed teeth to grab animals such as lemmings

DOUBLE-GLAZED FUR
The Arctic fox's white winter fur is made up of hairs which are hollow inside, full of air. The air in the hairs traps body warmth from the fox in much the same way as a double-glazed window traps warmth from houses. Air is a good insulator and does not let heat pass through it easily. The Arctic fox can tolerate temperatures of -40°C (-40°F), or even lower, quite comfortably.

Survival of the fittest

Pale maidens
Sisyrinchium filifolium

Flowers are
both male
and female

Capsules
contain seeds

ONLY SPECIALIZED, HARDY PLANTS can survive the fierce winds, biting cold, thin soils, and short growing seasons of the polar lands. The most successful plants are the simple ones, like mosses, lichens, and algae. Arctic and Antarctic plants often grow in low compact cushions or tussocks to keep out of the freezing, drying winds, to trap available moisture, and to avoid being crushed by snow and ice. In the short summer, flowers burst out and rapidly produce seeds before the winter weather returns. There are few insects in these cold places, so many plants reproduce from small pieces of themselves like runners or bulbils.

Plant is low
growing to
keep out of
the wind

Long roots
obtain
nitrogen
and water
in dry,
harsh
conditions

Root system
gives strong
anchorage

Arctic wormwood
Artemisia borealis

WELL ANCHORED
The northern primrose, *Primula scandanavica*, produces many seeds in a capsule. This splits open and releases the seeds when they are ripe.

PALE MAIDENS
This sub-Antarctic plant of the iris family has grass-like leaves. It is able to store food in fleshy roots underground. This ability helps it to survive and grow quickly in spring.

Flower heads are
about 5–6 mm
(0.25 in) across

FAST FLOWERS
Calandria feltonii is native only to the Falkland Islands (or Malvinas). A succession of short-lived flowers open quickly when the sun shines.

Fleshy
leaves
store
water

Silky or hairless
leaves are
deeply divided

ARCTIC WORMWOOD
This hardy plant, which grows throughout the northern hemisphere, is sometimes known as Arctic wormwood. It grows in colonies on dry, rocky ridges and gravel banks.

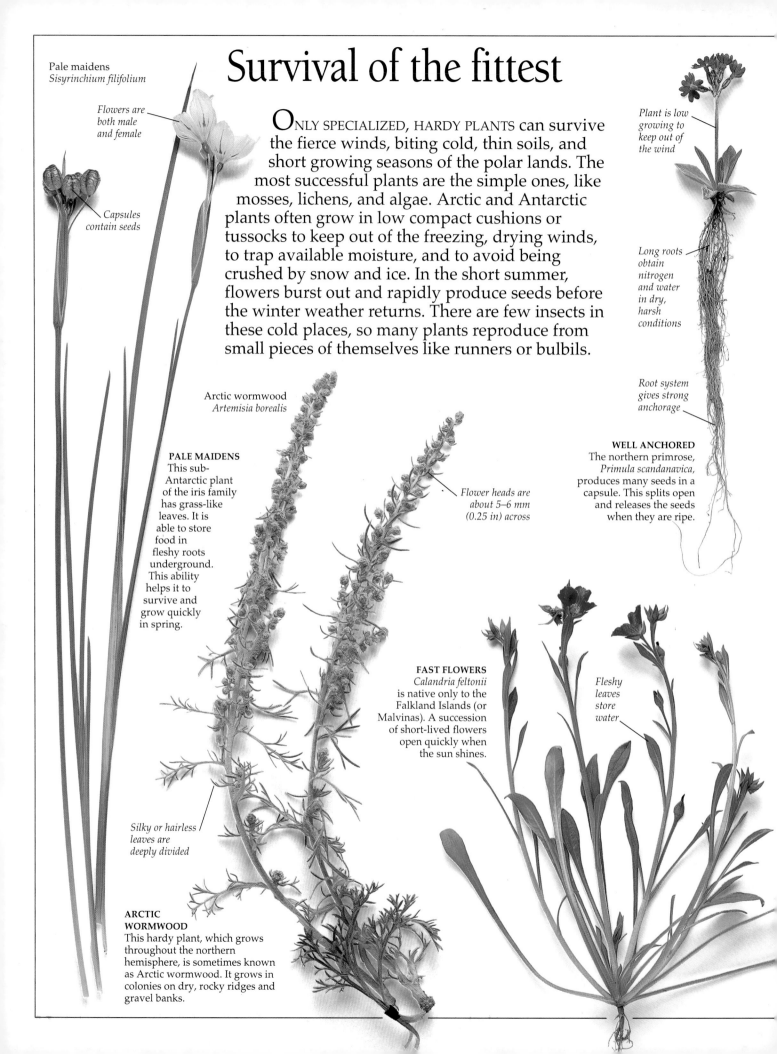

Woolly bear
caterpillar
Arctia caja

Northern fleabane
Erigeron borealis

INSECTS OF THE NORTH
There are several butterflies and
moths living in Arctic regions. The
hairs of the dark-coloured, fuzzy
caterpillars accelerate warming
and reduce heat loss.

*Branched
flower head
is called a
panicle*

*Side branches
have spikelets
on stalks*

*Daisy-like
flowers made
up of small
flowers
called florets*

Slipper-flower
Calceolaria fothergillii

INSECT REPELLANT
Low cushions of northern fleabane flower
in the Arctic summer when the tundra lands
become waterlogged and water collects on the
surface. The plant is highly unattractive to fleas
and midges, hence its name, and it is used
successfully by humans as an insect repellant.

*Large, lower
petals look
like a slipper*

*Flower sticks
out from leaves
so insects can
spot the flower
easily*

GROWTH OF GRASS
The most successful
plants in the cold polar
regions are the low
lying mosses and
lichens. However
several grasses
thrive in the Arctic,
like *Deschampsia
cespitosa*. On the
Antarctic mainland
only one grass
survives; *Deschampsia
flexuosa*, or Antarctic
wavy-hair grass.

*Hairy leaves
trap warmth
and moisture*

SLIPPER-FLOWER
This rare and beautiful slipper-flower
grows along the coasts of the Falkland
Islands. The colour of the large, slipper-
like lower petal attracts insects. While
feeding on the plant's nectar, pollen sticks
to them and is carried to another slipper-
flower which helps it to reproduce.

TREELESS TUNDRA
The tundra, a vast zone lying between the
ice cap and the timber line of Europe, Asia,
and North America, is the habitat for many
species of plants. The harsh climate and severe
winds dictate that low-lying plants predominate
and there are no trees. To take advantage of the
short summer, some plants complete their
whole life cycle in as little time as possible.

Birds of the Arctic

LIKE A BIRD
In 1926, the airship *Norge* carried
Norwegian Roald Amundsen and Italian
Umberto Nobile over the North Pole.

HAPPY FAMILIES
The little auk (*Alle alle*) is not much bigger than
a thrush, but there are a lot of them! Over 100
million little auks (or dovekies) breed along
Arctic coasts each summer. In winter, they
move south but usually stay near the Arctic
circle. Little auks have a thick layer of fat
under the skin to keep warm. They feed
on the rich supply of plankton in
the sea, storing food in a
throat pouch.

Few birds can survive the hostile Arctic climate all year
round, but residents include the ptarmigan, raven, ivory
gull, and little auk. The plumage of Arctic birds is more
dense than that of migratory species, especially in the
winter, and their feet, protected by feathers, do not freeze
to the ice. Most Arctic birds, such as waders, ducks,
geese, and swans, are migrants. Some migrants,
particularly waders, travel long journeys in winter, as far
as South America, South Africa, and Australasia. In
summer, Arctic birds take advantage of the rich insect
and small mammal life on the tundra, nesting and
rapidly rearing young before the winter sets in.
Many different types of birds can feed and nest
in close proximity because they share out the
available food; for instance, ducks eat water
plants, sea birds fish, and waders insects.

*Straight,
powerful beak
for stabbing
prey*

*Long neck to probe
in water beds*

ON DISPLAY
Cranes mate for life and perform
spectacular courtship dances, head
bobbing, bowing, skipping and sometimes
leaping as high as 6 m (20 ft) in the air.

*Streamlined, torpedo-shaped body
for swimming fast underwater*

RED HEADS
Sandhill cranes (*Grus canadensis*) breed mostly in the
remote Arctic, laying their eggs in mounds of grass or
other plants in an undisturbed marsh. Young birds
stay with their parents for nearly a year. The
sandhill crane's plumage often appears
rusty because of reddish iron oxide
stains from the water of tundra
ponds. The birds probe with
their bills in the mud for
worms, water creatures,
and frogs, then
transfer the stain
to their feathers
when preening.

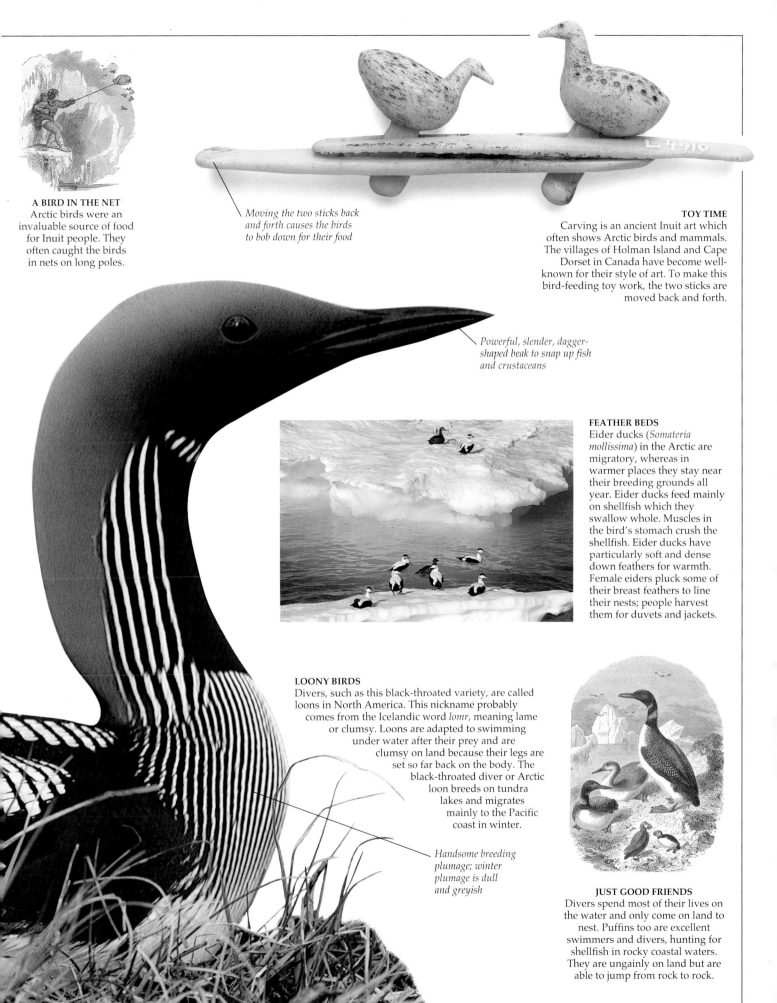

A BIRD IN THE NET
Arctic birds were an invaluable source of food for Inuit people. They often caught the birds in nets on long poles.

Moving the two sticks back and forth causes the birds to bob down for their food

TOY TIME
Carving is an ancient Inuit art which often shows Arctic birds and mammals. The villages of Holman Island and Cape Dorset in Canada have become well-known for their style of art. To make this bird-feeding toy work, the two sticks are moved back and forth.

Powerful, slender, dagger-shaped beak to snap up fish and crustaceans

FEATHER BEDS
Eider ducks (*Somateria mollissima*) in the Arctic are migratory, whereas in warmer places they stay near their breeding grounds all year. Eider ducks feed mainly on shellfish which they swallow whole. Muscles in the bird's stomach crush the shellfish. Eider ducks have particularly soft and dense down feathers for warmth. Female eiders pluck some of their breast feathers to line their nests; people harvest them for duvets and jackets.

LOONY BIRDS
Divers, such as this black-throated variety, are called loons in North America. This nickname probably comes from the Icelandic word *lomr*, meaning lame or clumsy. Loons are adapted to swimming under water after their prey and are clumsy on land because their legs are set so far back on the body. The black-throated diver or Arctic loon breeds on tundra lakes and migrates mainly to the Pacific coast in winter.

Handsome breeding plumage; winter plumage is dull and greyish

JUST GOOD FRIENDS
Divers spend most of their lives on the water and only come on land to nest. Puffins too are excellent swimmers and divers, hunting for shellfish in rocky coastal waters. They are ungainly on land but are able to jump from rock to rock.

Birds of the Antarctic

THE MOST COMMON Antarctic birds are seabirds such as penguins, albatrosses, and petrels, which come ashore in summer to breed in remote, predator-free locations. They take advantage of the seas around Antarctica, which are packed with food for hungry chicks. Only 13 species of flying birds make use of ice-free land for nesting on the Antarctic mainland. The rest squash into colonies on equally cramped sub-Antarctic islands. Antarctic birds rely on their dense feathers and frostbite-resistant feet to keep warm, while fat reserves in the skin act as both food reserves and insulation. Most Antarctic birds leave during the cold winter months. But some, including emperor penguins, king penguins, and wandering albatrosses, stay behind to complete their long breeding cycle. Others, such as sheathbills, only just manage to survive in the freezing winter conditions.

ANTARCTIC SCAVENGERS
Giant petrels are nicknamed "stinkers" because of their unpleasant smell. They use their powerful, hooked beaks for feeding and scavenging as well as killing other birds. Petrels will eat almost anything, including dead seals and whales. A petrel is about the size of a vulture, with a wingspan of nearly 2 m (6.5 ft).

Wings are held up like a Viking helmet, making the bird appear large and fierce

Ear-splitting shriek warns enemies to keep away

Powerful hooked beak to stab and kill prey

Wings are spread to display white patches

PIRATES OF THE SKIES
Peculiar, dog-like barking calls signal the arrival of a pair of skuas. Skuas live up to their reputation as "pirates of the skies" by chasing other birds, forcing them to regurgitate their food. These large, aggressive birds are also notorious for stealing the eggs and young of other birds, Two skuas may even cooperate while hunting, using clever tricks to snatch a meal more easily.

Antarctic skua
Catharacta maccormicki

Brown skua
Catharacta lonnbergi

NOT FUSSY
Sheathbills are the only land birds able to scrape a living in Antarctica. Their success is due to their varied diet, which includes penguin and seal feces, penguin eggs, chicks, dead fish, krill, and limpets. Sheathbills also steal food intended for penguin chicks.

Horny sheath protects nostrils

Orange growths at base of beak become brighter during breeding season

Jagged, hooked bill helps to grip slippery fish

Blue-eyed shag
Phalacrocorax atriceps

Wings are spread out to dry off after a swim

Feathers soak up water and allow the shag to dive more easily

Tern

Albatross

Shearwater

Cormorant

Penguin

DIFFERENT STROKES
The pursuit of a fishy meal involves a different technique for every type of bird. Cormorants use their strong feet to paddle deep underwater after prey, while penguins deep dive then propel themselves through the sea using their wings. A tern picks fish by plunging down just under the surface of the water, while albatrosses float on the surface keeping a sharp eye out for any likely food. Shearwaters spot their prey from the air and then plunge in pursuit.

SEAWEED NEST
Blue-eyed shags nest in smelly, noisy colonies close to the sea, building untidy nests of seaweed, lichens, mosses, and feathers glued together with guano (bird excrement). Blue-eyed shags breed on the Antarctic peninsula and on a number of Antarctic and sub-Antarctic islands. Some use their nesting sites all year round, roosting there throughout the winter. This allows them to stay near their fishing grounds in the open water.

Lords of the skies

THE HUGE SUMMER BREEDING COLONIES of birds in both the Arctic and the Antarctic attract a number of predatory birds quick to enjoy the easy meals of eggs and chicks. In the Arctic, the small mammals of the tundra lands, such as lemmings and hares, increase the range of food for birds to hunt. The variety of predatory birds is therefore greater in the Arctic than in the Antarctic and includes eagles, skuas, owls, falcons, and buzzards. The predators time their own breeding cycle to coincide with that of their prey, to ensure that their chicks will always have plenty to eat.

Snowy owl
Nyctea scandiaca

GHOSTLY HUNTER
Snowy owls feed largely on the millions of lemmings living on the Arctic tundra, and their population is closely linked to the regular three to four year rise and fall in lemming numbers (pp. 36–37). Many of these superb owls wander far south in winter.

Soapstone and ivory owl carved by Inuit craftsman in Cape Dorset, Canada

Feathers at tips of wings spread out like fingers to help the eagle push and steer through the air

Spread feathers help the bird to reduce speed

Lethal curved talons grip, crush, and carry off prey

Powerful wings give both speed and control in flight

Strong legs to cushion impact of landing

The golden eagle slows in mid-air and spreads out its wings and tail to act as a brake

Eyes firmly focused on its destination, the eagle further brakes its flight by swinging out its lower body and legs

At the last moment, its feet swing down to grip the perch

WATCH OUT BELOW
Golden eagles fly at low altitudes while hunting, then swoop suddenly to pounce on their prey. This swoop-and-grab attack is effective because it happens so swiftly that the prey is often taken unawares. Here, a golden eagle is landing on a branch in much the same way as it would when diving for its next meal.

KING OF THE CLOUDS
As the most powerful and majestic bird in the sky, the eagle features in countless stories, myths, and legends. Here, a magnificent eagle perches in a tree in an illustration by British illustrator Reginald Knowles. It forms the title page of a collection of Norse legends.

Golden eagle
Aquila chrysaetos

Keen eyesight to spot birds and animals moving on the ground below

Powerful hooked bill to tear flesh from prey

Huge chest muscles drive the enormous wings

Feathers down to toes to keep warm

Gyrfalcon
Falco rusticolus

A KILLING MACHINE
A magnificent flier, the golden eagle is a fierce predator of ptarmigan and other birds as well as small mammals such as ground squirrels and hares. Golden eagles usually kill their prey before carrying it off in their strong talons. They sometimes hunt in pairs, especially in winter.

FALCON FOOD
The rock ptarmigan (*Lagopus mutus*) is the gyrfalcon's main prey.

BIGGEST AND BEST
The most powerful of the falcons, the gyrfalcon relies on power and speed to catch its victims. They usually kill their prey in flight.

25

Ocean wanderer

THE HUGE, GENTLE ALBATROSSES of the Antarctic seas come ashore only to breed. They do not breed on the Antarctic land mass itself but on islands such as South Georgia, just north of the pack ice. There are six species of albatross breeding in the Antarctic: the black-browed, grey-headed, wandering, yellow-nosed, sooty, and light-mantled sooty. Probably about 750,000 pairs of birds breed each year, the main advantage of these isolated locations being safety from predators. Albatrosses raise only one chick at a time and the chick takes a long time to mature, sometimes remaining in the nest for up to a year. Chicks are protected from the intense cold by thick down feathers and an insulating layer of fat or blubber. When winter sets in, most albatrosses set off over the southern oceans once more.

A man weighed down by more than grief: albatrosses can weigh up to 12 kg (26 lb)

DEAD WEIGHT
Sailors believed albatrosses brought them good luck. In Coleridge's *The Rime of the Ancient Mariner*, the unlucky mariner is forced to wear an albatross he has killed.

Wings very long and slender for effortless gliding above the ocean

Black-browed albatross
Diomedea melanophris

BUMPY LANDING
Landing is a difficult task for a bird so well adapted to flying over the sea. When albatrosses approach the nest site, they circle round several times, before putting their legs down, like the landing gear on an aircraft. But they often land with a bump.

Webbed feet held wide to push against the air and act as brakes

Grey-headed albatross
Diomedea chrysostoma

Large eyes indicate sharp eyesight necessary for spotting food in the sea

BIRD MAN
People have always wanted to fly like birds but this design for an early flying machine was no challenge to the albatross's mastery of the air. For birds, as with planes, take-off and landing are the most dangerous parts of flying. Like planes, albatrosses need a runway to gather enough speed for take-off. Without this, their enormous wingspan and body weight ensure that they remain earthbound.

Tube-shaped nostrils have glands at the base that excrete excess salt

Bill has razor-sharp edges to catch fish and squid

LIVING THE HIGH LIFE
Grey-headed albatrosses live on steep cliff sides because they need the strong winds rising up over the cliffs to help them take off. Although grey-headed albatrosses weigh half as much as wandering albatrosses, only half of their chicks survive because the parent birds cannot obtain enough food to keep the young alive.

FAITHFUL FLYING ACE
The wandering albatross has the greatest wingspan of any living bird. Its wing power enables the bird to cover as much as 500 km (300 miles) a day, alighting on the sea to feed or in calm weather. Like all albatrosses, it comes ashore only to breed. The breeding cycle is exceptionally long, taking a year to complete. It therefore breeds only every two years. It precedes breeding by an elaborate courtship display, in which the two birds dance face to face making a variety of weird sounds, and clapping their beaks together loudly. Wandering albatrosses usually pair for life. The most elaborate displays take place among newly formed pairs; old established partners are more discreet.

Wingspan may be between 254–360 cm (8 ft 4 in– 11 ft 10 in)

During courtship the bird points its beak to the sky and moos like a cow

SECOND-HAND FOOD
Parent albatrosses feed their young by regurgitating (bringing up) the seafood they eat in the form of a sticky, oily mixture. This takes place when they return to the nest after many hours, or even days, fishing out at sea. Both adults and young can use this smelly and sticky oil in defence, ejecting it with reasonable accuracy over a couple of metres (6 ft) range. Predators, such as skuas, may be repelled by the foul smell or immobilized if the sticky oil saturates their feathers.

Mother feeds regurgitated krill to chick

Nest is lined with grass and feathers

Nest is about 30 cm (12 in) high

BARREL NEST
The black-browed albatross makes a raised nest of mud and straw among the tussock grass.

Strong legs and wide feet assist landing and swimming

Wandering albatross
Diomedea exulans

South Pole penguins

MILLIONS OF PENGUINS gathered at their noisy summer breeding colonies are one of the most spectacular sights of the Antarctic. Only two species, the Adélie and the emperor, breed on the Antarctic continent itself, but the gentoo, macaroni, chinstrap, rockhopper, and king penguin all breed within Antarctic waters. Emperor and king penguins lay a single egg; the other species usually lay two eggs each year. Penguins are supremely well adapted for swimming in cold seas. Some of these adaptations, particularly the dense, waterproof feathers and thick fat layers under the skin, also serve them well on land. The penguins rely on the fat as a store of energy when they are looking after eggs and chicks and cannot get out to sea to obtain food for themselves.

Short beak has feathers along part of its length for extra warmth

SAFETY IN NUMBERS
Penguins breed in huge, densely packed colonies called rookeries. Some rookeries contain millions of birds.

A PRACTICAL PENGUIN
Adélies winter out at sea off the pack ice but march inland to their breeding colonies in October. They navigate partly by means of the sun. Adélies usually return to the same mates and nest sites every year. They lay eggs in November and by February the chicks go to sea.

Powerful oar-like flippers propel penguin through water

Stiff tail of pointed feathers used as rudder in water and support on land

Torpedo-shaped body allows the penguin to slice through the water

Oily feathers overlap like roof tiles, providing a waterproof layer for the thick down feathers beneath

PERFIDIOUS PENGUIN
An evil penguin stars in the Oscar-winning British animated film, *The Wrong Trousers*. The treacherous penguin leaves a trail of havoc behind it as it attempts to remove a priceless jewel from a museum. Penguins are not, however, generally famed for their participation in diamond heists!

Adélie penguin
Pygoscelis adeliae

Short legs are set far back on body for steering while swimming

PADDED PENGUINS PARASCENDING
Tough feathers, a flexible skin, and thick blubber protect these penguins from knocks as they hurl themselves on to rocky shores or ice floes.

King penguin *Aptenodytes patagonicus*

Rockhopper penguin *Eudyptes chrysocome*

Gentoo penguin *Pygoscelis papua*

Powerful beaks to grasp slippery fish and other creatures

MARK OF DISTINCTION
The main distinguishing marks of penguins are on the head and upper breast so the birds are visible when they swim on the surface. The colours and head crests are used for species recognition and for courtship displays.

KING PENGUINS
Kings have golden-orange patches on their ears and bill. The long bill is useful for catching speedy fish and squid.

GENTOO PENGUINS
The pink bill of gentoos is dagger-shaped to catch fish and krill. Gentoos can swim at speeds of up to 27 km (16 miles) per hour.

ROCKHOPPER PENGUINS
Rockhoppers have conspicuous yellow eyebrows which they use for courtship display. They are the smallest polar penguin.

CHICKS AT RISK
Weak and sickly chicks, or those on the edge of the colonies, are most likely to fall victim to predators such as the skua (right).

NOISY NESTERS
Chinstrap penguins are good climbers, using their beaks and sharp claws to reach nest sites in high rocky places. They are noisy and aggressive penguins. They often take over the nesting sites of Adélies or steal stones from each other's nests.

Black feathers form a "chinstrap" across white breast

Shallow nest hollow lined with stones and vegetation

Chinstrap penguin *Pygoscelis antarctica*

Emperors of the Antarctic

IN EARLY APRIL, when most of Antarctica's wildlife heads north, the emperor penguin begins its 100 km- (60 mile-) trek south to reach its traditional nesting sites on the sea ice. The female lays her egg in early May and returns north to the open sea. The male then undertakes an incredible feat of endurance, incubating the egg alone through the icy winter. Because the egg cannot survive on the ice, the male incubates it on his feet. He therefore cannot feed and may lose up to half his body weight. The female returns to feed the chick when it hatches in July. To reach the breeding colony, and to leave it, the birds must cover a huge area of seaice in pitch darkness. Emperors rear a chick each year but only about one in five survive.

FEET HEAT
Chicks stand on the adults' feet until they are about eight weeks old, hiding under a brood pouch, or flap of skin for extra warmth and protection. Older chicks rely on their dense, fluffy feathers and the warm bodies of fellow chicks to keep warm, while their parents search for food.

TRULY MAJESTIC
The largest penguin, the emperor is about 1.15 m (nearly 4 ft) tall, and weighs 30 kg (66 lb). It can spend up to 18 minutes underwater and dive to over 260 m (850 ft).

The birds in the centre are the warmest of the group

A tightly packed group can reduce heat loss by as much as 50 percent

Birds take turns to occupy the most exposed positions

Emperors tend to turn their backs on the constantly shifting wind

TOGETHERNESS
Incubating males huddle together for warmth, moving very little in order to conserve energy. When the chicks are born the birds still huddle together as much as possible. Some emperor colonies contain over 20,000 pairs.

After the females have returned the emaciated males make their way to the open sea

Penguin "flies" out of the water to draw breath

Penguin catches fish and krill in its beak

Underwater, penguin steers with its feet and tail

Penguin shoots onto land or ice in giant leap of up to 2 m (6 ft)

DUCKING AND DIVING
Penguins "fly" through the water propelled by their stiff flippers. When swimming fast, they often use a technique called porpoising, leaping out of the water like dolphins or porpoises. Air offers less resistance to movement than water, so porpoising penguins can travel at speeds of 30 km (18 miles) per hour.

Bill is small to cut
down on heat loss

Emperor penguin
Aptenodytes forsteri

*In the nasal
cavities, much
of the warm air
normally lost
in breathing
is recycled*

*Closely packed,
overlapping
feathers cover a
thick layer of
blubber*

Feet are small
to cut down
on heat loss

King of the Arctic

THE POLAR BEAR IS THE LARGEST and most powerful hunter of the Arctic; an average male weighs as much as six adult people. There are probably 20,000 polar bears wandering over the vast Arctic ice floes; some of them even roam as far as the North Pole. Polar bears are solitary animals except in the breeding season. They do not hibernate and in the long winter when the Arctic pack ice extends further out to sea, they hunt for seals beneath the ice. Their dense fur keeps them warm even in the most severe conditions. An undercoat of thick fur is protected by an outer coat of long guard hairs. These hairs stick together when they get wet, forming a waterproof barrier. Under the fur, a thick layer of blubber performs two roles, insulating the bear against the cold, and acting as a food store to help the bear survive hard times.

The small rounded ears lose little body heat

Mature female polar bear
Thalarctos maritimus

HEAVYWEIGHT
An average adult male polar bear measures 2.5 m (8 ft) from head to tail and weighs about 500 kg (over 1,000 lb). The largest males grow up to 3 m (10 ft) in length and can weigh up to 900 kg (2,000 lb). Female polar bears are much smaller than the males.

Female keeps floor clean by covering it with freshly scraped snow

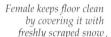

Strong teeth for killing prey

BEARING ARMS
Play helps to strengthen cubs and lets them practise the skills they will need when they are adults. Young bears often wrestle in the snow with their mouths wide open to show off their sharp teeth. Such fights rarely result in injury. Finding and killing prey is hard and bears have developed a bad reputation for raiding human settlements in search of food.

Air vent scraped in roof lets stale air escape

Female first digs the tunnel then hollows out the chamber

CAVE CUBS
Polar bear cubs are born in December or January in a warm cosy den dug in the snow by their mother. The cubs grow rapidly on their mother's rich milk, which is about 30 percent fat. While in the ice cave the mother has nothing to eat and lives on the stored fat in her body.

CAPABLE CLIMBER
In spite of their huge size, polar bears are quite able to climb trees, such as this one at Cape Churchill on Hudson Bay in Canada. Between 600 and 1,000 bears gather here in October to wait for the bay to freeze over so that they can head out over the ice to hunt.

Thick fur prevents bear from being scratched

Back legs are especially strong

POLAR PADDLE
Polar bears are very good swimmers. They swim slowly but strongly, and can keep swimming for days. They use only their front legs to swim, while the back legs are held still like a rudder.

SEAL SLAYER
Polar bears are clever and patient hunters. Over 90 percent of their diet consists of seals. They wait by a seal's blow hole in the ice, pouncing as soon as it comes up for air. One stroke of the bear's massive paw and a bite at the back of the skull kills the seal. Most hunting trips are unsuccessful and a bear may not eat for five days.

Yellow-white fur acts as camouflage

Powerful legs to outrun prey

Hollow hairs trap warm air near body

Thickly padded soles covered by rough skin and sometimes tough hair

Sharp claws for grabbing prey

Non-slip soles help grip slippery ice

The mighty moose

THE MOOSE IS THE LARGEST MEMBER of the deer family. It stands up to 2.4 m (over 7 ft) high and can weigh up to 825 kg (1,815 lb). The moose can be found throughout northern Canada and the United States, and in northern Europe and Asia, where it is sometimes called elk. In Europe and Asia the moose lives mainly in the coniferous forests bordering the tundra, but in North America it ranges widely over the tundra, spending long periods on the shores of the Arctic ocean in mid-summer, when flies are likely to plague it further inland. When winters are particularly harsh, moose often move further south in search of food, to areas which have lighter snow cover. Moose are very solitary animals and their population density is low; because of their immense size they need a relatively large area to themselves to enable them to find an adequate food supply. However, in winter when in search of new food supplies, they will often travel in a group, covering considerable distances.

Flat shape gives moose a stable surface with which to push rivals

The bell is a fold of skin covered with hair

LETHAL WEAPONS
The bull moose has heavy, flattened antlers. These are used for fighting rival males during the breeding season, rather than for protection. The moose sheds its antlers every year and grows a new set. By late August the antlers are fully grown, and the bull strips off the "velvet" covering and polishes his great weapons against a tree.

*Moose
Alces alces*

Under surface of moose's foot

SURE FOOTED
The moose has long and sharply pointed hoofs, in contrast to those of its relative the reindeer which are rounded. The pointed hoofs help the moose grip the ice and snow.

Calf remains close to mother for several months

Reddish-brown coat becomes darker as the calf matures

Long legs allow even young moose to walk easily through deep snow

MAKING MORE MOOSE
The mating season of the moose lasts from four to eight weeks in the autumn. The bull wanders around looking for and calling females (cows); the cows return the calls. The bull will follow every sound to see if it was made by a cow or a rival bull. Baby moose are born in late May and June. The mother carries the baby for about seven and a half months before the birth. There is usually one calf, although twins and even triplets are not uncommon. When the calf is about ten days old it can travel with its mother. The bull will then remain by himself or join other males.

Antler spread can be as much as 2.05 m (6 ft 8 in)

Antlers are not fully grown and are still heavily covered with velvet

MONEY MOOSE
The moose is such a revered animal in many north European countries that it has even featured on banknotes. This note comes from Lithuania.

Muzzle hangs 8–10 cm (3–4 in) over its chin

Short neck, coupled with long legs, mean that moose has to get on its knees to eat low-growing plants

SOLITARY GIANT
The preferred habitat of moose is tundra land containing willow swamps and lakes. Moose are fine swimmers and can cross lakes and rivers with ease. They like to roll in mud holes which helps to get rid of any small parasitic animals. In summer, they eat leaves and tender twigs as well as grass and herbs. Because of their great size and dangerous antlers they have few natural predators, with the exception of humans. Wolves may occasionally attack isolated moose and young, although the antlers of the adult make it a formidable foe.

Arctic willow *Salix arctica*

FAVOURITE FOOD
Arctic willow (*Salix arctica*) and Alaska willow (*Salix alaxensis*) are the favourite foods of the moose.

Moose is beginning to lose the velvet on its antlers

WATER WADERS
Moose are often to be found standing up to their knees in water. This helps them to get rid of the flies which trouble them greatly in the warm summer months, but they also feed on the aquatic vegetation. An adult will consume up to 19.5 kg (43 lb) of vegetation a day. Sometimes they retreat into water to escape predators such as wolves.

Tundra wildlife

THE ONLY ANIMAL that can live on the Arctic pack ice is the polar bear. However, several animals live on the Arctic tundra (pp. 8–9), both as residents and migrants. During summer in the Arctic a great deal of the ice on the tundra melts, plants begin to flourish, and insects hatch out. This means that there is suddenly plenty of food for animals that have spent all winter on the tundra, as well as for the migrants who arrive as soon as the snows melt. Because the sun never sets in the Arctic in summer (pp. 6–7), the animals can feed all through the night. It is necessary for them to do this so that the young can grow as quickly as possible, because the summer is short and the land soon freezes over again.

TUNDRA VEGETATION
The tundra consists of a nearly continuous, although at times thin, cover of vegetation dominated by grasses like the Arctic cottongrass (*Eriophorum angustifolium*) seen here. Scattered among the grasses are various mosses, a variety of flowering herbs, and a few species of dwarf shrubs and willows.

Limit of permanent ice
Limit of drift ice
Tree line
Tundra

Arctic Circle
Canada
Arctic Ocean
Greenland
Russia

SEA OF ICE
The central area of the Arctic Ocean remains permanently frozen. The tundra, which spans North America and Eurasia is covered in snow and ice in winter, but is verdant in summer. No trees grow on the tundra because it is too cold and windy even in the summer months.

Long, pointed ears enable the lynx to hear well in dense, muffling snow

FELINE VISITOR
The Arctic lynx (*Lynx canadensis*) is mainly a creature of the forest which borders areas of the tundra in North America, but they are often to be found in the true tundra during the summer months. Their brown coat blends well with the tundra landscape in summer, and in winter the coat becomes thicker and lighter so that the lynx is hard to see against the snow.

In winter big feet are covered with thick fur which acts like a snowshoe

Snowshoe hare
Lepus americanus

HARE LINE
Three types of hare inhabit the tundra – the snowshoe hare, the rare Alaskan hare, and the common Arctic hare. Hares grow white winter coats and have well-developed claws which enable them to dig through the snow for food.

The lemming is very common on the tundra

MASS SUICIDE?
Every few years, when their numbers outgrow their food source, lemmings (*Lemmus sibiricus*) become restless and a mass migration begins. They press on madly, often passing food sources, until they reach the sea, where many are drowned.

TURNCOAT
The stoat or ermine (*Mustela erminea*) changes its coat from brown to white in winter, and is protected from harsh weather by living beneath the snow. It is an attractive animal, but a ruthless hunter. Ermines' slimness enables them to pursue lemmings, their main prey, through the lemmings' networks of underground tunnels.

GREAT BEAR
The word Arctic comes from the Greek word *Arctikos* meaning "pertaining to the constellation of the bear". The extensive star constellation Ursa Major, the Great Bear, is visible only in the northern hemisphere.

GLUTTON OF THE ARCTIC
The wolverine (*Gulo gulo*), a distant relative of the stoat, looks like a smallish bear. Wolverines are solitary animals and usually meet others only to mate during the summer. Hoods made from their coats appear not to collect ice crystals, so wolverine fur is much prized. The wolverines' main prey is reindeer. Although much of the flesh is eaten on the spot, wolverines hide away the remainder for another day, earning themselves a reputation for gluttony.

Sometimes the fur is tipped silvery white

Bears have sensitive noses and a strong sense of smell

Powerful jaws and teeth allow bear to eat a variety of foods

SLEEPYHEAD
The brown or grizzly bear (*Ursus arctos*) lives in the tundra regions of Alaska and Canada and in some parts of Russia. They eat a wide variety of small mammals, fish, insects, and plants according to the season and the area in which they live. In the winter months the grizzly digs a snug den in the ground and hibernates, taking approximately two weeks to enter a deep winter sleep. During hibernation the body temperature drops and the bear lives off its reserves of stored fat. They sometimes sleep for as long as seven months.

Long claws on the front paws help the bear to dig

Bears often stand upright on the soles of their back feet

37

Reindeer and caribou

REINDEER ARE CALLED CARIBOU in North America. The name "caribou" may come from *xalibu*, the native American Micmac word for "the animal that paws through snow for its food". Wild reindeer still survive on the frozen tundra of North America, Scandinavia, and Siberia, but they have also been domesticated in Scandinavia and Siberia for thousands of years. Although their thick coats insulate them against the Arctic cold, they migrate south in the winter to find food and shelter. As they travel, they grow a thicker, greyer winter coat. In summer, reindeer are plagued by hordes of insects, such as mosquitoes and warble flies, as they graze on the tundra meadows. Their main predator is the wolf; this natural population regulation is necessary to enable the surviving reindeer to find sufficient food in a decreasing habitat.

REINDEER STAR
The most famous reindeer in the world is probably red-nosed Rudolph, one of the reindeer pulling Father Christmas's sleigh.

TITLE FIGHT
In the autumn mating, or rutting, season, bulls with their antlers locked together wrestle to decide which are the strongest. The winners of these contests collect groups of cows for mating and then defend their harems from all comers.

Antler buds appear two weeks after the old ones are shed

New antlers are covered by soft, thick velvet

Fully-formed antlers are bone hard

BIG, BIGGER, BIGGEST
Antlers are shed each year. Bulls shed their antlers at the end of the year, while the cows wait until spring. New antlers grow rapidly and are fully grown by the start of the autumn rutting season.

Nuclear explosion

NUCLEAR POLLUTION
In 1986 a nuclear reactor at Chernobyl in the Ukraine exploded. Lichens absorbed radioactive Caesium 137 from the nuclear fall-out. Reindeer ate the lichens making them ill and their meat unfit to eat.

Reindeer moss (*Cladonia* species) absorbed radioactivity from the air

Velvet contains blood vessels to nourish the growing antlers

LICHEN LUNCH
Reindeer feed largely on lichens, which are one of the few foods available throughout the Arctic winter. Some reindeer living on Arctic islands will also eat seaweed. In summer a wider variety of plants are available. Adult reindeer eat about 4.5 kg (10 lb) of food a day to get the energy they need.

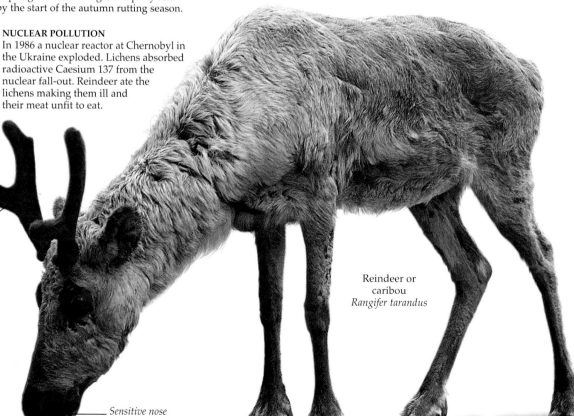

Reindeer or caribou *Rangifer tarandus*

Sensitive nose helps reindeer to find food even under the snow

CEREMONIAL APRON
This shaman's ceremonial apron was made from reindeer hide. The shaman was a powerful figure in the culture of many Siberian and North American tribes since it was believed he could obtain power from the supernatural beings that were everywhere on land, and even lurked beneath the sea.

Iron symbols of the sun, fish, and diving birds decorate apron

Heat is lost rapidly through antlers in velvet, cooling the reindeer on hot summer days

Hollow hairs contain air which traps body heat

Iron-bladed reindeer skin scraper used by Siberian Tungus tribe

SWIMMING CHAMPIONS
Migrating reindeer have to cross many fast-flowing rivers. They are strong swimmers, plunging into the icy waters without any hesitation. The reindeers' broad feet help them to swim strongly against the current, and the hollow hairs in their coats help them to float more easily.

Lapp stick with spade-like blade to probe under the snow for food

Muzzle covered with fine, warm hair

TOOLS OF THE TRADE
Many Scandinavian and Siberian peoples relied on the reindeer for food, clothing, and shelter. They devised many tools specifically to enable them to take full advantage of their domesticated animals.

Dense, waterproof coat turns grey-white in winter

Broad feet fringed with fur stop reindeer sinking into snow

Sharp hooves grip ice and dig through snow for food

GROWING UP FAST
Calves are born in June and grow fast on their mother's rich milk, which is four times as nutritious as cow's milk. Calves can keep up with the movements of the herd when they are one or two days old, and are better protected from predators such as wolves if they remain within its safety. Calves stay with their mothers for about a year, growing their first antlers when they are around two months old.

Company of wolves

BLENDING INTO THE BACKGROUND
In the Arctic areas of North America and Eurasia, wolves often have white coats for camouflage. Because the animals they hunt cannot see them easily, the wolves can get really close to their prey. In the forests to the south of the tundra, the wolves have grey or even blackish fur.

WOLVES ARE INTELLIGENT AND ADAPTABLE animals that survive in the chilling Arctic cold thanks to their thick fur and co-operative hunting techniques. They generally live in packs of between eight and 20 family members. They are bonded together by affection for each other, and a ranking system of near military precision. Pack members establish their rank at almost every meeting: a dominant or high-ranking wolf stands erect, ears and tail pointing upwards, and may show its teeth, then growl. A subordinate or low-ranking wolf crouches, holds its tail between its legs, and turns down its ears; instead of growling, it whines. A wolf pack ranges over a specific area, picking off sick, aged, or injured herd animals. Needlessly feared and persecuted by humans for thousands of years, wolves kill only to survive, and do not deserve their bad reputation – they are in fact the ancestors of all domesticated dogs.

RING OF HORN
Wolves are expert hunters and prey chiefly on large hoofed animals such as caribou, moose, and musk oxen. To defend themselves from a wolf pack, a herd of musk oxen form a tight circle, with the wolves on the outside and the females and young in the centre. By panicking the musk oxen, the wolves can break the circle and reach the calves inside. But if a wolf is caught by one of the musk oxen's horns, it can be tossed into the air and then trampled.

Two-layered coat with soft, dense underfur and long, outer hairs to keep out the cold

Mouth remains wide open during howling

Wolf throws back its head in order to howl

Wolf
Canis lupus

LEADER OF THE PACK
The wolf's instinct for power and freedom has inspired countless writers. The American novelist Jack London wrote his novel *The Call of the Wild* after spending a year in the Yukon in Canada. It is the story of Buck, a domestic dog who becomes wild and eventually leads a wolf pack.

IN HARMONY
An eerie howl in the night echoes through countless horror films, striking terror into the hearts of the audience. In fact, howling is simply one of the ways in which wolves communicate with each other. Wolf-speak ranges from whimpers and growls to complex facial and body expressions. Wolves howl in order to keep in touch with pack members, or to warn other packs to keep out of the area. If one wolf howls, the others join in, often harmonizing with each other. The variety of sound makes the pack seem bigger and more formidable.

Sensitive ears can track sounds
up to 3 km (2 miles) away

Poor eyesight means wolf
must rely on superb hearing
and sense of smell

Long muzzle hides powerful jaws
and teeth for killing prey and
tearing flesh; 42 teeth include
sharp canines for gripping prey

Wolves have
as many as 17
different facial
expressions

Grey wolf
Canis lupus

THE WOLF WITHIN
Jack London's novel *White Fang*,
set in the Yukon in Canada, is
the story of a wolf domesticated
to become a pet. In practice, it is
virtually impossible – and illegal
– to keep wild wolves as pets.

BORN TO BE WILD
Wolves are superbly adapted to Arctic life.
Their keen sense of smell and hearing has
been honed to perfection for tracking down
their prey. They have evolved strong bodies
and long legs for chasing their quarry. Agile
and graceful, they can jump up to 4.5 m
(15 ft) and can leap upwards, sideways, and
even backwards, like a cat. Just like dogs,
wolves walk on their toes and have large
pads with claws that do not retract. This
allows them to run fast on flat ground while
keeping their footing on rocks, ice, and other
slippery surfaces.

Wolves can sleep out in the
open tundra, although they
often find a snow hole or a
cave in which to shelter

The weighty walrus

HUGE, UNGAINLY, AND ENORMOUSLY FAT, the walrus, a close relative of the seal, has superbly adapted to its Arctic lifestyle. A thick layer of blubber (fat) keeps the animal warm. Four flat flippers make the walrus an excellent swimmer, as well as allowing it to shift its heavy bulk on land. Female walruses give birth in the spring, usually on boulder-strewn beaches. The female usually produces a calf every other year, and cares for her young for about two years – twins are very rare. Walruses follow the seasonal ebb and flow of the Arctic ice, migrating as far as 3,000 km (1,900 miles) north every time. In the process, the animals must negotiate polar bears and killer whales, their greatest enemies other than humans.

WORLD-FAMOUS WALRUS
Lewis Carroll (1832–98) included in his famous story *Alice Through the Looking Glass* a walrus and a carpenter. They invite some oysters to walk with them – and then eat them. In real life, walruses eat mainly shellfish, and bivalves like clams.

THE CALL OF LOVE
Walrus courtship is an elaborate process. A male seduces a female with barks, growls, and whistles. If she is impressed by his love song, she will slip off with him and mate in the water. These two walruses are tenderly rubbing moustaches prior to mating.

Thick skin on neck and shoulders protects the walrus during fights

Tusks can grow up to 1 m (3 ft) long

Broad front flippers can support heavy body on land

Walrus
Odobenus rosmarus

FURRY FRIEND
Just like the much smaller catfish, walruses have a row of coarse but very sensitive whiskers. The whiskers grow constantly to make up for daily wear and tear. The walrus uses this delicate moustache to search for invertebrates on the murky ocean floor.

HEAVYWEIGHT
Weighing in at around 1 tonne (2,200 lb), this formidable male walrus surveys his domain. Females are only slightly smaller – they tip the scales at 0.85 tonne (1,900 lb).

AN INTIMATE ARRANGEMENT
Walruses are intensely sociable animals. During the summer, enormous groups of walruses lie around on the land, packed together in large, noisy groups. Keeping close conserves body heat, as well as making it harder for a predator to pick off an individual animal.

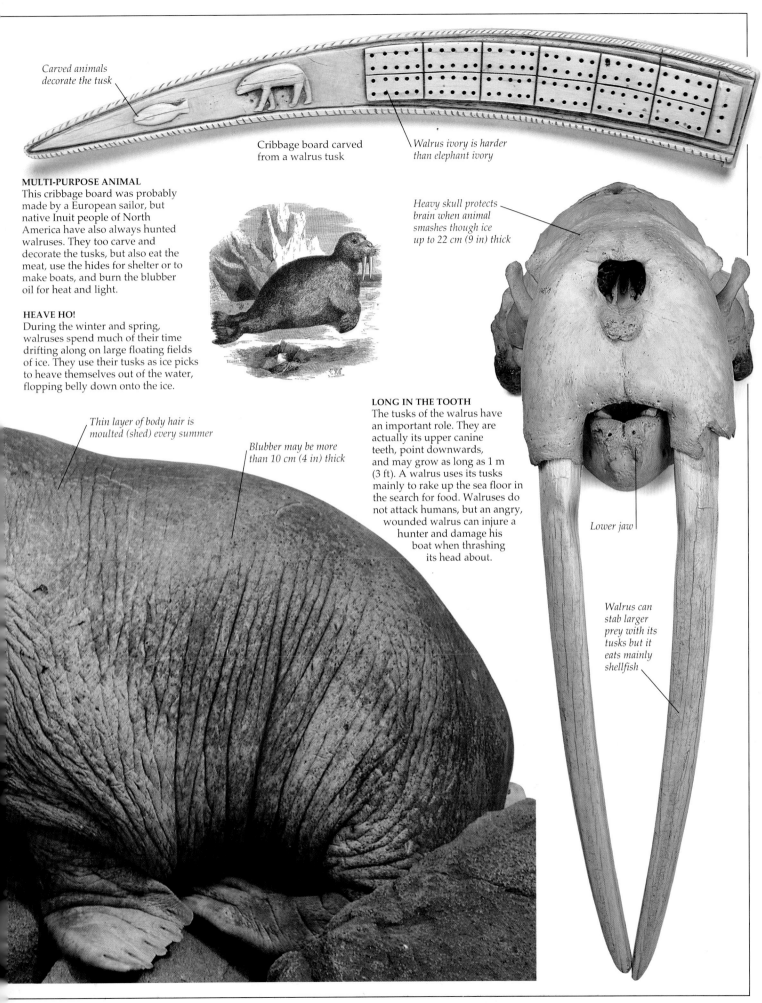

Carved animals decorate the tusk

Cribbage board carved from a walrus tusk

Walrus ivory is harder than elephant ivory

MULTI-PURPOSE ANIMAL

This cribbage board was probably made by a European sailor, but native Inuit people of North America have also always hunted walruses. They too carve and decorate the tusks, but also eat the meat, use the hides for shelter or to make boats, and burn the blubber oil for heat and light.

HEAVE HO!

During the winter and spring, walruses spend much of their time drifting along on large floating fields of ice. They use their tusks as ice picks to heave themselves out of the water, flopping belly down onto the ice.

Heavy skull protects brain when animal smashes though ice up to 22 cm (9 in) thick

Thin layer of body hair is moulted (shed) every summer

Blubber may be more than 10 cm (4 in) thick

LONG IN THE TOOTH

The tusks of the walrus have an important role. They are actually its upper canine teeth, point downwards, and may grow as long as 1 m (3 ft). A walrus uses its tusks mainly to rake up the sea floor in the search for food. Walruses do not attack humans, but an angry, wounded walrus can injure a hunter and damage his boat when thrashing its head about.

Lower jaw

Walrus can stab larger prey with its tusks but it eats mainly shellfish

43

Suited to the sea

SEALS ARE PROBABLY the hardiest of all the Arctic and Antarctic mammals. The ringed seal of the Arctic and the Weddell seal of the Antarctic both survive below the ice during the dark winter months. Other seals, such as the Arctic harp seal, migrate into polar waters as the warmer summer weather arrives. All seals have to leave the water to rest, give birth, and mate. In contrast to their graceful swimming in the sea, seals move clumsily on land, wriggling and sliding across the ice with some difficulty. Seals usually give birth in late winter. By spring the pups are strong enough to start making the most of the fish and rich food supplies of the polar waters. Fur seals and sea lions have problems coping with the heat of an Arctic or Antarctic summer. Their fur and blubber causes them to overheat, and the seals have to pant, flap their flippers, or cover their bodies with sand or mud to cool down. Seals have been hunted for their fur and blubber for hundreds of years; they are also threatened by the increasing pollution of the oceans.

Guard hairs protect the seal as it slides over rocks

Dense underfur traps warm air

TWO FUR COATS
Fur seals have two kinds of hair in their coat. Long guard hairs on the outside form a protective layer, while fine underfur stops body heat escaping. Many seals have hairless bodies, and depend on their blubber for warmth.

ICY WINTERS
Weddell seals (*Leptonychotes weddelli*) spend the whole winter under the Antarctic ice sheet, gnawing at the ice with their teeth to keep open air holes for breathing. In summer, the seals move onto the ice or rocks. Pups are born in September and October, and can swim at about six weeks. Weddell seals make a wide range of sounds underwater, possibly for locating prey or blowholes, or to communicate with other seals. They can dive to depths of about 580 m (1,900 ft), and stay submerged for up to 70 minutes.

BALLOON NOSE
Male hooded seals (*Cystaphora cristata*) have an inflatable balloon-like structure at the end of their nose. This is blown up when the seal is excited or in danger, and may serve to warn off rivals or enemies.

The male has a huge swollen nose like an elephant's trunk

JOBS FOR THE BOYS
Gigantic male southern elephant seals (*Mirunga leonina*) roar defiance to their rivals in the breeding season, using their extraordinary nose like a loudspeaker. The female gives birth to a single pup, which she suckles for about a month. During this period she will not feed, existing instead on energy reserves in her blubber. Males do not eat during the breeding season either, since they are constantly defending a harem of females against rival males.

Male elephant seals are up to ten times heavier than females

While it is suckled the pup may quadruple its weight in three to four weeks.

HIDDEN DEATH
Inuit hunters sometimes hide behind white shields mounted on small sledges as they hunt seals.

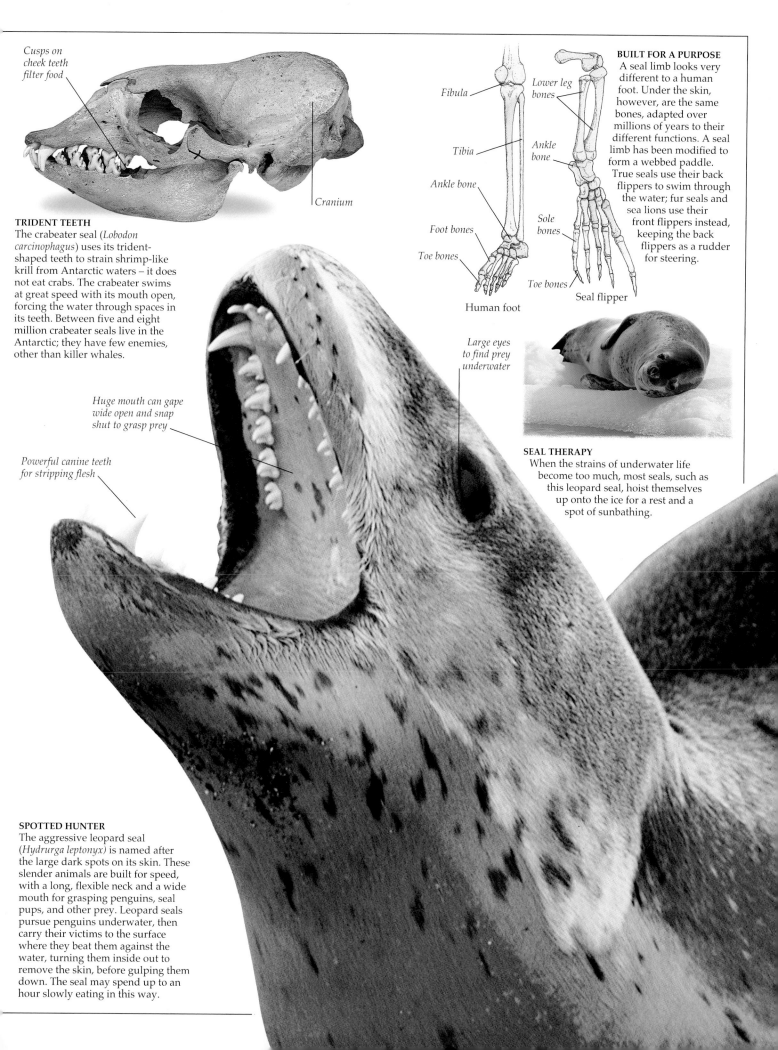

Cusps on cheek teeth filter food

Cranium

TRIDENT TEETH
The crabeater seal (*Lobodon carcinophagus*) uses its trident-shaped teeth to strain shrimp-like krill from Antarctic waters – it does not eat crabs. The crabeater swims at great speed with its mouth open, forcing the water through spaces in its teeth. Between five and eight million crabeater seals live in the Antarctic; they have few enemies, other than killer whales.

Huge mouth can gape wide open and snap shut to grasp prey

Powerful canine teeth for stripping flesh

BUILT FOR A PURPOSE
A seal limb looks very different to a human foot. Under the skin, however, are the same bones, adapted over millions of years to their different functions. A seal limb has been modified to form a webbed paddle. True seals use their back flippers to swim through the water; fur seals and sea lions use their front flippers instead, keeping the back flippers as a rudder for steering.

Fibula

Tibia

Lower leg bones

Ankle bone

Ankle bone

Foot bones

Sole bones

Toe bones

Toe bones

Human foot

Seal flipper

Large eyes to find prey underwater

SEAL THERAPY
When the strains of underwater life become too much, most seals, such as this leopard seal, hoist themselves up onto the ice for a rest and a spot of sunbathing.

SPOTTED HUNTER
The aggressive leopard seal (*Hydrurga leptonyx*) is named after the large dark spots on its skin. These slender animals are built for speed, with a long, flexible neck and a wide mouth for grasping penguins, seal pups, and other prey. Leopard seals pursue penguins underwater, then carry their victims to the surface where they beat them against the water, turning them inside out to remove the skin, before gulping them down. The seal may spend up to an hour slowly eating in this way.

Giants of the seas

THE POLAR SEAS are home to a whole range of whales. The grey, humpback, fin, and blue whales are summer residents, making good use of a rich supply of plankton. When winter comes, and the krill disperse to graze beneath the pack ice, most of the whales migrate to warmer waters near the equator. The narwhal, beluga, and bowhead whales remain in the Arctic all year round, while minke whales survive the Antarctic winter. Whales do not feed much during the winter, relying on body fat to sustain them. Whales began to disappear when people hunted them for profit from their oil, baleen (whalebone), and meat. Now that commercial whaling has declined, many whale populations have recovered.

INUIT CARVING
This Inuit model of a sperm whale comes from Alaska. Whalers were much influenced by Inuit carving when they began to engrave the teeth and bones of whales.

Epidermis

Dermis

Blubber can be 25 cm (10 in) thick

Connective tissue

Fascia

Muscles

HOT FAT
Under a whale's skin there is an insulating layer of fatty blubber. A network of blood vessels runs through it. If the whale overheats, more blood is pumped up nearer to the cold water to cool the whale down.

SEA UNICORN
The spiral tusk of the male narwhal (*Monodon monoceros*) is an elongated tooth. Tusks were traded before people outside the Arctic had seen narwhals and may have led to the legend of the unicorn.

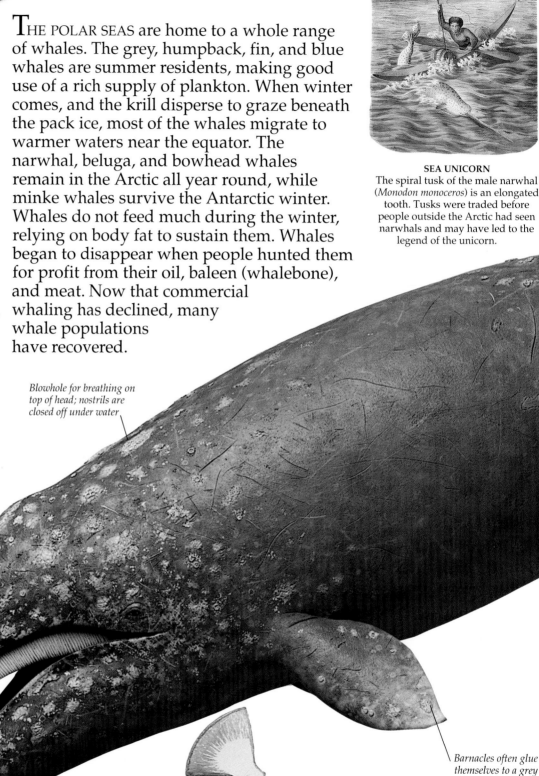

Blowhole for breathing on top of head; nostrils are closed off under water

About 150 pairs of yellowish-white baleen plates filter plankton

ONE LONG HOLIDAY
Grey whales make the longest migration journeys of any whale. They winter off the coasts of California and Mexico, then swim to their Alaskan feeding grounds for the summer, a round trip of more than 20,000 km (12,000 miles). Grey whales only feed in the summer, living off stores of energy in their blubber for the rest of the year. The young are born in the warmer waters of their winter home.

BONEFINGER
Inside a whale's flipper are the same bones as in our own hands. Flippers are used for steering and braking; the tail gives the swimming power.

Barnacles often glue themselves to a grey whale's skin and hitch a ride around the oceans

CLEVER KILLERS
Killer whales (*Orcas*) live in pods of 4–40 individuals which hunt together. They are the fastest mammals in the sea, able to reach 56 kph (35 mph). They even tip seals off ice floes and snatch sea lions from beaches. Nothing is safe from them, not even a blue whale.

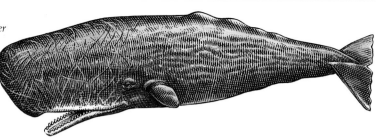

CHAMPION DIVER
The sperm whale (*Physeter catodon*) can easily dive down to about 350 m (1150 ft) and stay under for 10 minutes or so. Some do far more. The longest recorded dive is 90 minutes, and dives may reach 3,000 m (10,000 ft).

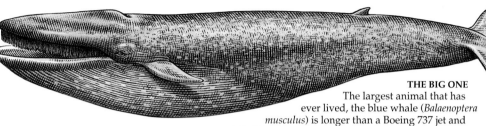

THE BIG ONE
The largest animal that has ever lived, the blue whale (*Balaenoptera musculus*) is longer than a Boeing 737 jet and weighs 25 times more than an African elephant. Blue whales are now rare, having been brought close to extinction by commercial whaling.

Row of 6–14 humps on back instead of dorsal fin

Large, strong muscles in the tail power the flukes. About a third of a whale's body is pure muscle

Flat, rigid tail flukes, stiffened with cartilage, move up and down to push the whale through the water

Killer whale

Fish   Seal   Seabird   Minke whale

Squid

Krill

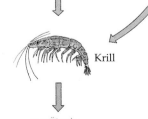

Plankton

Top attaches to whale's upper jaw

NATURAL BALANCE
Killer whales are the top carnivore in many sub-Arctic and sub-Antarctic food chains, and a vital part of the food webs of polar seas. Their prey includes fishes, seals, penguins, and other whales. Fishermen are often in conflict with killer whales because they feel the whales take valuable fish stocks. But the whales are part of the natural balance of life in the oceans, easily upset by people over-fishing.

GIANT SIEVES
Some whales, such as the right whales, grey whale, humpback whale, and blue whale, sieve food from the sea water with fringed brushes, called baleen, inside their mouths. These whales have huge, arched jaws from which the baleen plates hang like curtains. Like fingernails, baleen is made of a substance called keratin.

A herding life

PEOPLE HAVE SURVIVED in the inhospitable Arctic regions of northern Scandinavia and the northern regions of Siberia for thousands of years. Native Arctic peoples followed a hunting and fishing lifestyle, adapting to the intense winter cold, darkness, and snow without the aid of modern technology. Starvation and death by exposure were constant threats. Native peoples of the Eurasian Arctic include the Saami or Lapps of northern Scandinavia, and the Chukchi, Evenks, and Nenets of Siberia and northeastern Asia. Some Chukchi families still follow wild reindeer herds, herding or lassoeing them for their meat and pelts. Reindeer provided Arctic peoples with all their basic needs, such as food, clothing, tents, tools, and items to trade. In some remote areas, the native peoples still manage to follow a traditional hunting lifestyle. But many now work in villages or towns, with some combining the old and new ways of life.

Staff is made of iron

SPIRIT POWER
In many traditional Siberian societies, a specially trained *angakok*, or shaman, acted as the link between the supernatural and natural worlds. A shaman fulfilled many roles, from doctor and meteorologist to performer of miracles. This shaman's headdress is embroidered with reindeer hair.

Shaman's head ornament from Siberia

HANDY IN WINTER
This ivory carving of reindeer pulling a sledge comes from central Siberia. Many Siberian tribes used reindeer as pack and draught animals for carrying their household goods. Today, some reindeer herders hire out their reindeer sledge for transport during the winter.

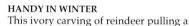

Foot represents a bear's paw

IN A TRANCE
Shamans of the Tungus tribe, east of the Yenisey river in central Siberia, held this staff while meditating. The shaman often went into a trance and spoke with the voice of a spirit "helper".

PACK YOUR BAG
The northern Komi lived in a region west of the Urals, in northeastern Europe. They filled this *patku*, or kit-bag, with clothes and other smaller items, and loaded it onto a baggage sledge when following reindeer herds.

Bag is made of stretched reindeer hide

Hide from different parts of the reindeer's body provide the changes of colour in the decoration

MOVING CAMP
As nomadic people might move several times a year, their tents had to be simple and lightweight as well as sturdy. The tents were usually based on a conical framework of wooden poles, covered with several reindeer skins. The top of the tent was left open to allow smoke from the fire to escape.

Nenet tent, Siberia

A great deal of heat is lost through the head so a hood is vital for keeping the head and ears warm in freezing conditions

Seams are very finely stitched to make the garment as warm and waterproof as possible

Nenet child's hooded winter parka

HUNTER OR HUNTED?
This hooded jacket from the Aleutian islands between Siberia and Alaska is made from strips of seal or walrus intestine, sewn together to make a waterproof garment. By dressing in the skins or fur of the animals, the hunter was making an important point – he became part of the animal world around him by taking on the appearance of both the hunter and the hunted.

Reindeer gut was often used for sewing skins together

Mittens are sewn right into the sleeves for extra warmth and protection

Fur trim was decorative, but also protected against icy winds

ORIGINS OF THE PARKA
A traditional winter coat of the Nenet tribe of northern Siberia consisted of a thick, warm, long-sleeved jacket called a parka. The coat was sewn together from pieces of reindeer skin. The reindeer hide was worn on the outside; for the inner clothing, softer fur was placed next to the skin for extra warmth. Woollen undergarments provided added protection, and helped to trap body heat. Some people still wear traditional clothes, but most buy winter clothes made of synthetic materials.

Hunters of the north

The model has a traditional hairstyle

Strips of white hide from under-side of caribou are used as decoration

Both men and women wore sealskin boots called kamiks

Inuit clothes were often heavily embroidered

INUITS, CALLED ESKIMOS by 19th-century Europeans, are the original inhabitants of the Arctic tundra of northern Canada, Alaska, Russia and Greenland. About 100,000 Inuits still live there. Inuits and related peoples were nomadic hunter-gatherers. They lived near the coast in summer, building up food reserves for the winter. The rest of the year they travelled, hunting caribou, seals, polar bears, and whales, and used every part of the animals they caught for food, shelter, clothing, tools and weapons. Inuit society was organized in extended family groups, with each member carrying out a specific job according to sex, age, and status. Games, storytelling, and music helped to pass the long winter hours. Most Inuits now live in permanent settlements and combine a regular job with hunting forays.

WINTER WARMTH
This traditional man's winter costume is made of caribou skin. Women sewed the skins together with sinew and a bone needle, and sometimes decorated the clothes with beadwork or embroidery. Only the families of good hunters had clothes that they replaced each year. Poor families unable to get autumn caribou skins wore their clothes for more than a year, or had to make their parkas out of sealskins.

ANCIENT ART
Inuits carved elaborate animal figures out of walrus ivory, caribou antlers, and whale or seal bone. They used ivory bow drills as instruments. This Inuit carving of a woman standing on a seal comes from Baffin Island. Today, Inuit artists use modern tools and soapstone to make carvings for tourists.

Only the tiniest area is exposed to the freezing air

Hunter pulled on line attached to harpoon to haul seal out of the water

Fitted tray holds leather harpoon rope

Sealskin jacket protected hunter from icy Arctic winds

A seal bladder float was attached to any large catch so that it would float behind the canoe

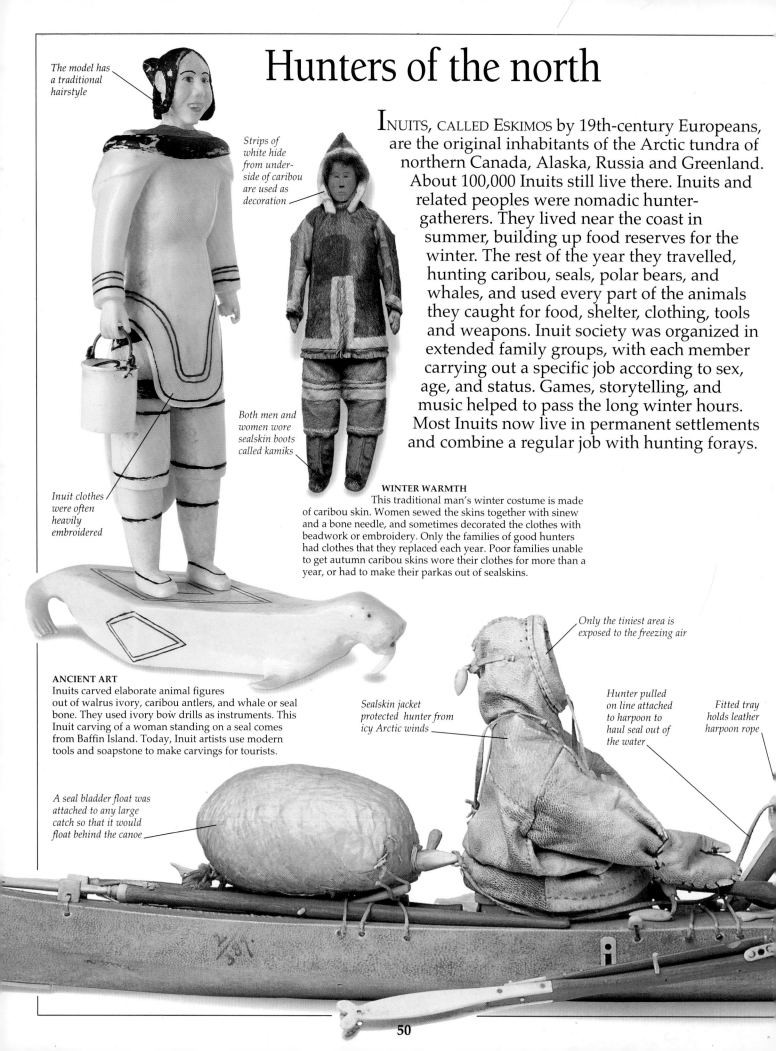

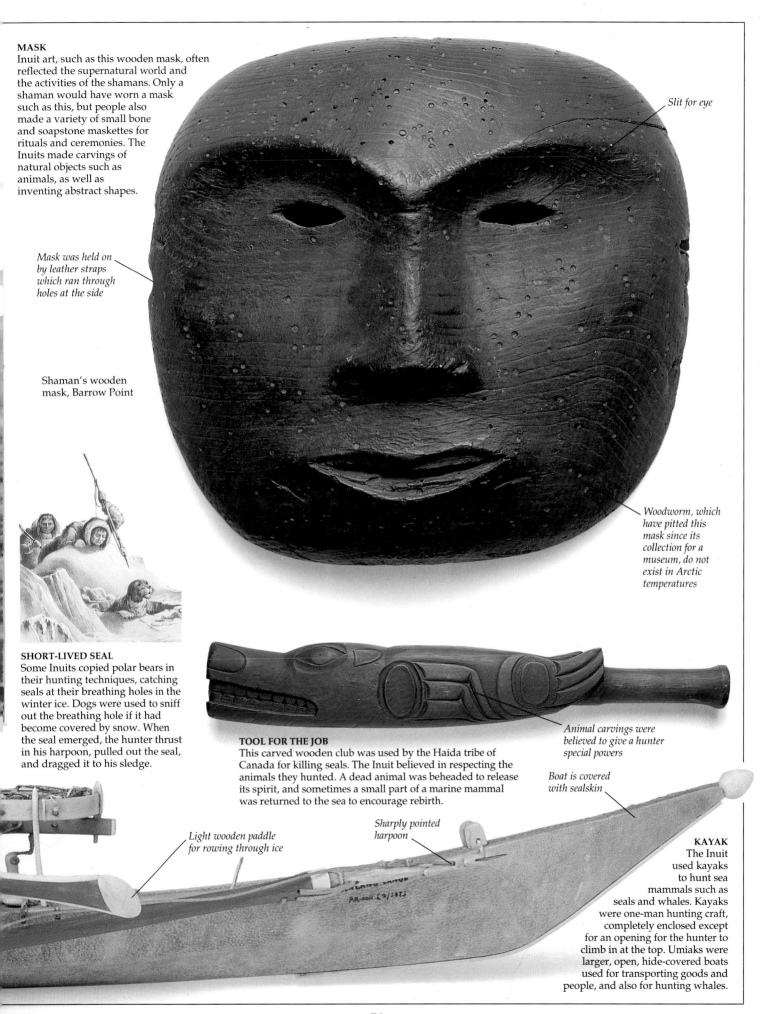

MASK
Inuit art, such as this wooden mask, often reflected the supernatural world and the activities of the shamans. Only a shaman would have worn a mask such as this, but people also made a variety of small bone and soapstone maskettes for rituals and ceremonies. The Inuits made carvings of natural objects such as animals, as well as inventing abstract shapes.

Slit for eye

Mask was held on by leather straps which ran through holes at the side

Shaman's wooden mask, Barrow Point

Woodworm, which have pitted this mask since its collection for a museum, do not exist in Arctic temperatures

SHORT-LIVED SEAL
Some Inuits copied polar bears in their hunting techniques, catching seals at their breathing holes in the winter ice. Dogs were used to sniff out the breathing hole if it had become covered by snow. When the seal emerged, the hunter thrust in his harpoon, pulled out the seal, and dragged it to his sledge.

TOOL FOR THE JOB
This carved wooden club was used by the Haida tribe of Canada for killing seals. The Inuit believed in respecting the animals they hunted. A dead animal was beheaded to release its spirit, and sometimes a small part of a marine mammal was returned to the sea to encourage rebirth.

Animal carvings were believed to give a hunter special powers

Boat is covered with sealskin

Light wooden paddle for rowing through ice

Sharply pointed harpoon

KAYAK
The Inuit used kayaks to hunt sea mammals such as seals and whales. Kayaks were one-man hunting craft, completely enclosed except for an opening for the hunter to climb in at the top. Umiaks were larger, open, hide-covered boats used for transporting goods and people, and also for hunting whales.

Discovering the Arctic

Norwegian flag

IN THE 15TH CENTURY, European powers, intent on trade expansion, sponsored voyages into uncharted waters. Much early European exploration was centred on the search for a northern sea route to China and India which would halve the time and danger involved in travelling overland. After the discovery of America, two routes were envisaged: the northwest passage following the American coast, and the northeast passage, along the Siberian coast. The search for the northwest passage was soon monopolized by the British and the French later joined by the Americans; the Dutch and the Russians concentrated on the northeast. Over the next 350 years explorers opened up the Arctic, but it was not until 1878 that a Swede, Adolf Nordenskjïld navigated the northeast passage, and 1905 when the great Norwegian explorer Roald Amundsen sailed through the northwest passage.

UP AND AWAY
Salomon Andrée, a Swedish aeronaut, and two companions, tried to reach the North Pole in the balloon *Örnen* (*Eagle*) in 1897. The balloon was weighed down by ice and forced to land. All three men perished.

Sir John Franklin 1786–1847

Fox collar

RESCUE FOXES
Eight foxes were released in the Canadian Arctic wearing collars bearing the name and position of a rescue ship, and medals were distributed among the local people. It was hoped they might encounter Franklin survivors.

Medal

THE SEARCHERS
In 1845 Sir John Franklin led 128 men on a search for the northwest passage. By 1847 nothing had been heard from them, and his wife mobilized many expeditions to hunt for them. In fact they had all died but the searches greatly advanced geographical knowledge of the Arctic.

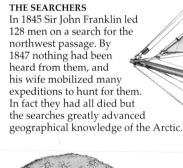

THE HOMECOMING
In 1818 John Ross (leading the procession), returned home to England having failed to find the northwest passage but having succeeded in killing a bear! This cartoon was by George Cruickshank.

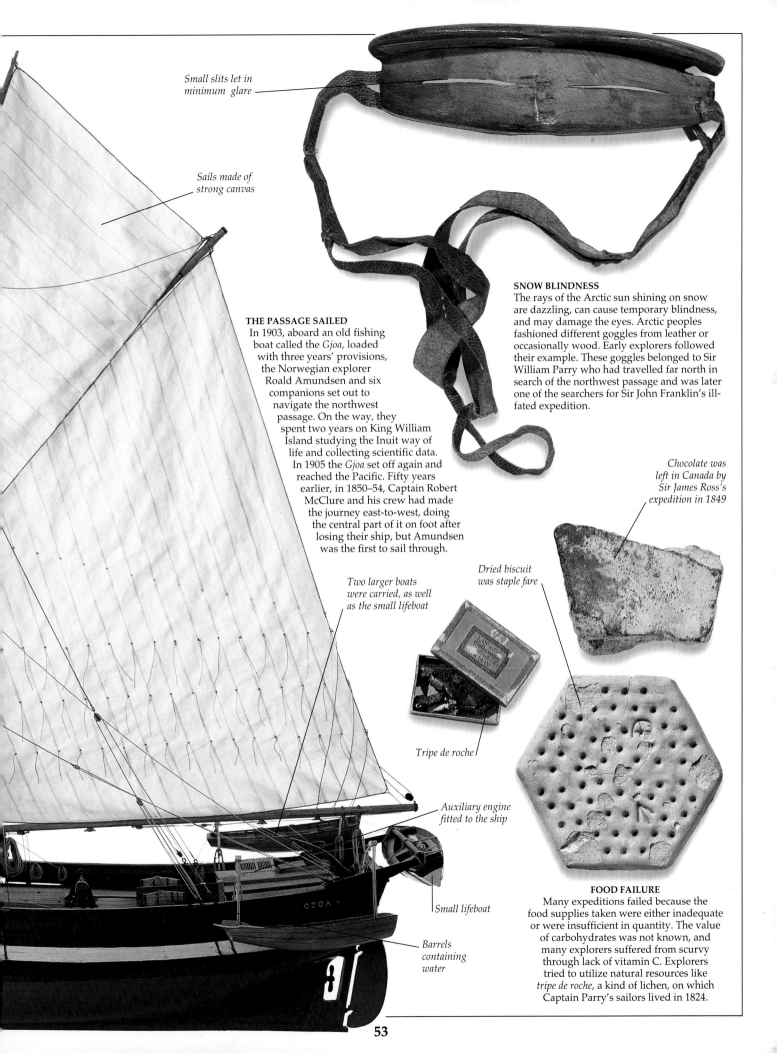

Small slits let in
minimum glare

Sails made of
strong canvas

SNOW BLINDNESS
The rays of the Arctic sun shining on snow
are dazzling, can cause temporary blindness,
and may damage the eyes. Arctic peoples
fashioned different goggles from leather or
occasionally wood. Early explorers followed
their example. These goggles belonged to Sir
William Parry who had travelled far north in
search of the northwest passage and was later
one of the searchers for Sir John Franklin's ill-
fated expedition.

THE PASSAGE SAILED
In 1903, aboard an old fishing
boat called the *Gjoa*, loaded
with three years' provisions,
the Norwegian explorer
Roald Amundsen and six
companions set out to
navigate the northwest
passage. On the way, they
spent two years on King William
Island studying the Inuit way of
life and collecting scientific data.
In 1905 the *Gjoa* set off again and
reached the Pacific. Fifty years
earlier, in 1850–54, Captain Robert
McClure and his crew had made
the journey east-to-west, doing
the central part of it on foot after
losing their ship, but Amundsen
was the first to sail through.

Chocolate was
left in Canada by
Sir James Ross's
expedition in 1849

Dried biscuit
was staple fare

Two larger boats
were carried, as well
as the small lifeboat

Tripe de roche

Auxiliary engine
fitted to the ship

Small lifeboat

Barrels
containing
water

FOOD FAILURE
Many expeditions failed because the
food supplies taken were either inadequate
or were insufficient in quantity. The value
of carbohydrates was not known, and
many explorers suffered from scurvy
through lack of vitamin C. Explorers
tried to utilize natural resources like
tripe de roche, a kind of lichen, on which
Captain Parry's sailors lived in 1824.

Scott and the Antarctic

Surveying
the land

AT THE BEGINNING of the 20th century, several nations wanted to explore the Antarctic. In 1910, Robert Scott (1868–1912) from Britain set out on his second Antarctic journey. As well as aiming to reach the pole, his expedition had scientific objectives. After using motor sledges, dogs, and ponies, and man-hauling sledges through the harsh terrain, Scott and his team, Wilson, Bowers, Oates, and Evans finally arrived at the pole only to find that the Norwegian explorer, Roald Amundsen had reached it weeks before them. On the return journey, the weather worsened and, weakened by cold and hunger, all five men perished. But although they lost the polar race, their scientific studies formed a new landmark in Antarctic science.

RUNNING REPAIRS
This sewing kit was taken by Dr. Wilson on Scott's ill-fated 1910–12 expedition. Keeping cotton and canvas clothing in good repair was essential in the harsh and difficult conditions.

Microscope magnifies the image inside the instrument

Compact and lightweight kit for travelling

Side mirror reflects light into the instrument

Günther & Tegetmeyer
BRAUNSCHWEIG, № 4716

BASE CAMP
From this desk in his "den" in base camp at Cape Evans, Scott wrote his diary, letters, and reports, studied maps, and planned the details of his trek to the pole. The extreme cold and the dry atmosphere have preserved the hut virtually as it was in 1910.

ELECTRIC SPIDER
This electrometer, taken by Scott to Antarctica, was used to measure minute fluctuations in atmospheric electricity. If there was a difference in electric charge between the earth and the atmosphere, a small suspended mirror inside the electrometer would move. This movement was compared against the fixed line of a suspended fine filament from a black widow spider's web.

Wire to earth the instrument

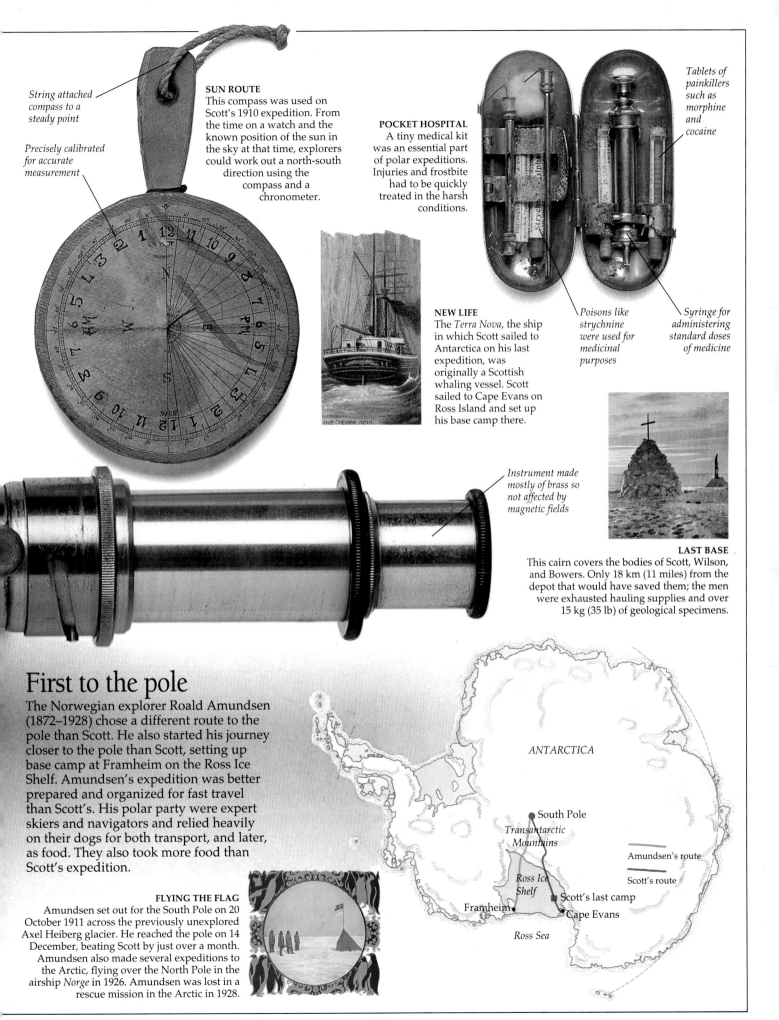

String attached compass to a steady point

Precisely calibrated for accurate measurement

SUN ROUTE
This compass was used on Scott's 1910 expedition. From the time on a watch and the known position of the sun in the sky at that time, explorers could work out a north-south direction using the compass and a chronometer.

POCKET HOSPITAL
A tiny medical kit was an essential part of polar expeditions. Injuries and frostbite had to be quickly treated in the harsh conditions.

Tablets of painkillers such as morphine and cocaine

NEW LIFE
The *Terra Nova*, the ship in which Scott sailed to Antarctica on his last expedition, was originally a Scottish whaling vessel. Scott sailed to Cape Evans on Ross Island and set up his base camp there.

Poisons like strychnine were used for medicinal purposes

Syringe for administering standard doses of medicine

Instrument made mostly of brass so not affected by magnetic fields

LAST BASE
This cairn covers the bodies of Scott, Wilson, and Bowers. Only 18 km (11 miles) from the depot that would have saved them; the men were exhausted hauling supplies and over 15 kg (35 lb) of geological specimens.

First to the pole

The Norwegian explorer Roald Amundsen (1872–1928) chose a different route to the pole than Scott. He also started his journey closer to the pole than Scott, setting up base camp at Framheim on the Ross Ice Shelf. Amundsen's expedition was better prepared and organized for fast travel than Scott's. His polar party were expert skiers and navigators and relied heavily on their dogs for both transport, and later, as food. They also took more food than Scott's expedition.

FLYING THE FLAG
Amundsen set out for the South Pole on 20 October 1911 across the previously unexplored Axel Heiberg glacier. He reached the pole on 14 December, beating Scott by just over a month. Amundsen also made several expeditions to the Arctic, flying over the North Pole in the airship *Norge* in 1926. Amundsen was lost in a rescue mission in the Arctic in 1928.

ANTARCTICA

South Pole

Transantarctic Mountains

Amundsen's route

Scott's route

Ross Ice Shelf

Scott's last camp

Framheim

Cape Evans

Ross Sea

Keeping warm and safe

FIGURE OF FUR
Amundsen's clothing was typical of that worn in the early 1900s.

EARLY EXPLORERS SUFFERED greatly because they did not know how to keep warm, and, equally important, dry, in harsh conditions. The freezing power of the icy winds was also largely ignored. Frostbite was very common and many men died of exposure. In time, lessons were learnt from the native peoples, and by the early years of this century, equipment had improved enormously. Expeditions used sleeping bags and fur boots and wore canvas jackets to protect themselves from the icy winds. Provision of essential foods was another factor which blighted many early expeditions. Too much emphasis was placed on the need for meat, and carbohydrates, vital for energy, were largely ignored. Today a great deal is known about the foods necessary for a healthy diet.

LAYER BY LAYER
The inadequacy of the clothes they wore contributed to the deaths of Captain Scott and his companions. They sweated a great deal, which froze, making the body cold and the clothes heavy and uncomfortable. Layers of lightweight clothes allow good ventilation and at the same time the trapped air insulates against the cold.

Polypropylene fabric takes moisture away from the body, preventing heat loss caused by sweat evaporation

Inner layer: "long johns" worn next to the skin

Potato

Bolognaise sauce   Shepherd's pie

Cooking vessel

Removable inner sole

TRAVELLING LIGHT
Travelling in the freezing polar landscapes is hard work whether on ski, by skidoo, or sledge. Food therefore has to be light and compact and quick and easy to prepare. Dried foods which only have to be mixed with heated ice or snow fulfil all the requirements and are also nutritious.

FEET FIRST
The feet and the hands are particularly vulnerable to frostbite so it is essential that these parts of the body are adequately covered. Today, different types of footwear have been designed for different conditions.

Thermal lining can be removed for easy drying

Padded sole for extra toughness

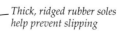

Glacier boots for use in deep powder snow

Adjustable lacing ensures a good fit

Thick, ridged rubber soles help prevent slipping

EYE SHADES
Goggles are worn
to protect eyes from
wind-blown snow
and harmful,
ultraviolet sun rays.

*Middle layer: fibrepile
undergarment traps a
layer of air which is
warmed by the body*

ICE CRACKER
When climbing steep
ice, two ice axes are
banged into the ice
face. The climber
then pulls up the
face on them.

*Zips allow garments
to be easily removed*

*Waterproof nylon
covering stops the
goosedown becoming
wet and losing
insulating
efficiency*

*Outer layer:
jacket*

*Adjustable wrists
prevent snow
entering mitt*

*Thermal inner
mitts are worn alone
when delicate outside
work is being done*

*Waterproof outer mitts
are lined with fibrepile
fabric for warmth*

POLAR MAN
One of the many advantages
of layer dressing is that the
number of layers can be
adjusted according to the
temperature and the activity
of the wearer. This outer
layer consisting of jacket and
salopettes is filled with high-
quality pure goosedown, which
is the most efficient of natural
fillings. Combined with the mid
and base layers, these garments
provide insulation sufficient to
keep warm at -40° C (-40° F).

*Outer layer:
salopettes*

*Crampons attached
to the soles
provide grip*

FOOT SUPPORT
These climbing boots are
made of strong and fairly
stiff plastic which supports
the foot and ankle. They have
a removable thermal lining.
Good footwear is essential
in polar conditions

*Thermal
socks worn
next to
the skin*

*Padded socks
add extra
warmth and
help keep
the feet dry*

Polar travel

THE SNOW AND ICE of polar regions have always posed special problems for people travelling about. Snowshoes and skis stop people sinking too far into soft snow, while boots with rough or spiky soles grip icy ground. Long, low sledges on smooth runners reduce friction and make it easier to move heavy loads over slippery, frozen surfaces. Early polar explorers learned from native Arctic peoples the benefits of using husky dogs to pull their sledges (Lapp people used reindeer for the same purpose). Modern motorised vehicles, such as the snowcat, with claw-like grips, or the skidoo, with skis underneath, were developed from tried and tested traditional forms of transport.

THE FIRST SNOWMOBILE
Scott's motorised sledge was the first vehicle with caterpillar tracks to be designed specially for snow. The slats on the tracks helped to grip the snow. The vehicle was far ahead of its time, but had an unreliable early petrol engine, and soon developed serious mechanical faults in the severe Antarctic environment. But it was a fore-runner of the snow scooters and skidoos of today.

POLAR HORSESHOE
The pressure of a horse's or pony's hooves drives straight down through the snow, causing them to sink up to their bellies. The hooves also break through sea ice and snow bridges very easily. Snowshoes for horses and ponies help to spread out the weight so they have more chance of staying on the surface.

"Tennis racket" shape to spread weight as evenly as possible

A BRAVE MAN'S SHOES
These snowshoes were worn by Captain Oates, who perished on Scott's 1910–12 expedition to Antarctica. Oates's feet became frost-bitten on the return journey, and then gangrenous. Rather than hold his companions up, he walked out of Scott's tent in a blizzard to die, so that they would be free to press on as fast as possible. His last words were "I am just going outside and may be some time." He hoped that this would enable his companions to save themselves but, tragically, his heroic gesture did not have the result he desired.

TOBOGGAN RUN
Sledges used in the Arctic and Antarctic need to be robust enough to carry heavy loads, but light enough for dogs or people to pull. Different types of sledge suit different conditions. Narrow runners are best for hard ice, wide runners for soft snow. This wooden sledge dates from 1934–37 and is loaded with scientific equipment and food and medical supplies. A team of 12 huskies can pull a fully loaded sledge weighing half a tonne.

Shovel for digging snow

Wooden runners with iron on top to make them stronger and more hard-wearing

Flat-bottomed sledge like a toboggan "floats" easily over the surface of the snow without sinking in too far

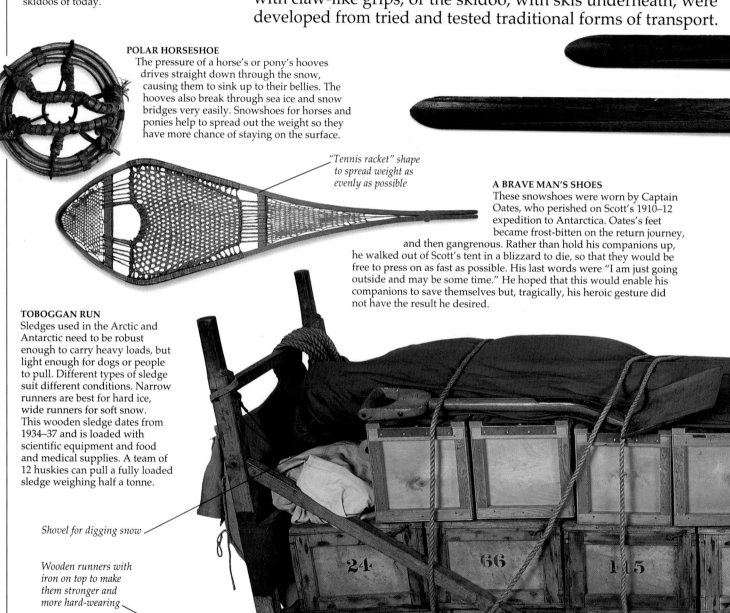

A RARE SIGHT
Today, few reindeer are harnessed to sledges or used as pack animals. Most Lapp families who keep reindeer have settled in large villages and do not follow their reindeer on migration journeys.

CANOEING THE SNOW
Traditional methods of travel in Lapland included various types of canoe-shaped sledges called pulkkas. These had one runner only and were usually pulled by reindeer. A common kind of pulkka was large enough for one adult passenger who sat with their legs outstretched, ready for braking. A wider pulkka was used to transport belongings. A third kind of pulkka was used by the Skolt Lapps for carrying sick people, children, and belongings. Reindeer were harnessed three abreast to this pulkka.

SMOOTH MOVERS
These heavy, wooden skis were used by Scott on his first expedition to Antarctica in 1901–04. Skis can be used on most kinds of snow and ice. They spread out the weight of a person, helping them to stay on the surface of the snow. They also reduce friction, sliding easily over snow and ice and allowing greater distances to be covered than by walking.

SNOW DOGS
The husky dogs used to pull sledges are social animals, working in a strict hierarchy under their leader in a sledge team. They are hardy, strong, and intelligent, but compulsive fighters. Huskies can survive freezing temperatures curled up in snowdrifts. The snow acts as an insulating blanket, helping to keep them warm at night or during blizzards.

Stout wooden cases loaded with scientific equipment, food, and medical supplies

Canvas cover for protecting supplies

"WITH CAPTAIN SCOTT AT THE SOUTH POLE"
Fry's PURE Cocoa & CHOCOLATE
MAKERS TO H.M. THE KING.

DRIVEN TO THE DOGS
Sledges pulled by dogs are one of the best means of moving heavy loads over ice and snow. Normally, it takes at least a year or two of hard practice to learn how to drive a dog sledge.

Life at the poles

THE CRUEL SEAS, savage, unpredictable climates, and inhospitable terrains of the two polar regions have ensured that neither environment has ever been completely conquered by humans. Indeed, the history of polar exploration is one of appalling hardship and a terrible toll of human life. However, in the Arctic, the Inuit peoples evolved survival skills over the centuries which enabled them to live a fruitful existence. European explorers learned much from their way of life and gradually applied this knowledge to their own ability to live in and explore these harsh environments. Today, the lifestyle at the poles for both Inuits and other polar dwellers is very similar. Scientific advances in clothing, transport, food, and building have ensured a way of life far removed from the privations of the past.

HELPING HANDS
Many early explorers died because they could not build strong enough shelters. By the 19th century Arctic explorers realized how much they could learn from the native peoples.

EFFICIENT RECYCLING
Edward Wilson, on Scott's last expedition, made a successful candlestick out of a biscuit tin. Explorers tried to find an alternative use for everything.

Entrance passage

Storage alcove

Window made from a block of freshwater ice

OVERNIGHT STAY
Today Inuits may still build igloos as temporary shelter. Here the hunter is lighting his primus stove with which he will warm himself and cook his dinner.

SNOW HOUSE
Contrary to popular belief, Inuits never built igloos as permanent homes but as temporary bases during the winter seal-hunting season. For much of the time they lived partly underground in dwellings made on a frame of driftwood or whalebone and covered by sods.

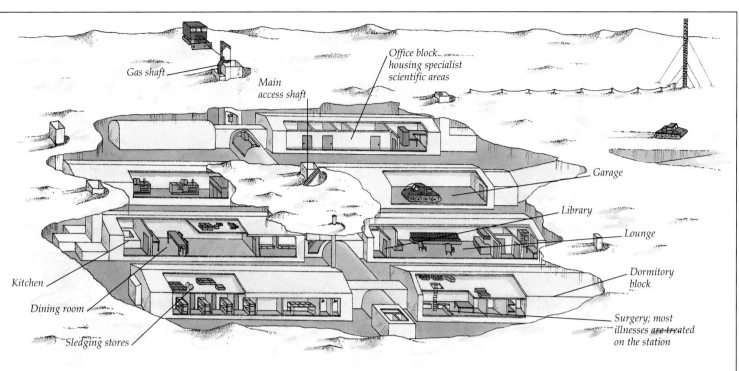

Gas shaft

Main access shaft

Office block housing specialist scientific areas

Garage

Library

Lounge

Dormitory block

Surgery; most illnesses are treated on the station

Kitchen

Dining room

Sledging stores

ALL MOD CONS

Today several countries have large research stations in the Antarctic, some permanent and some temporary. Most stations are involved in scientific surveys in geology, geophysics, glaciology, terrestrial biology, and atmospheric sciences. Several stations, like Britain's Halley Station, have been built underground. Halley has been replaced four times, as each of the successive structures has been crushed by the steadily shifting ice sheet.

SKIDDING AROUND

Polar travel is no longer reliant on dogs or ponies. Today most people travel on skidoos or snow-mobiles, which are small, motorised sledges on skis. They are easy to manoeuvre and can pull very heavy loads.

Blubber oil lamp

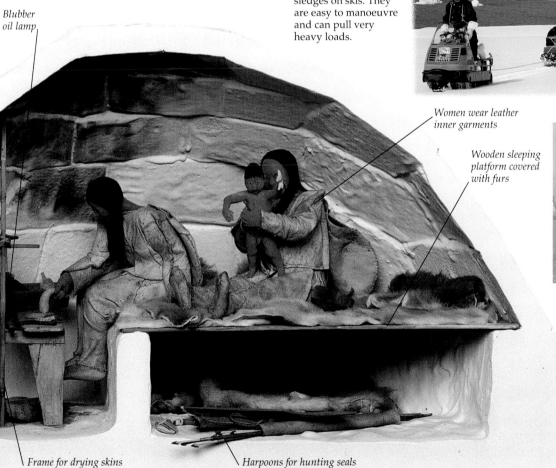

Women wear leather inner garments

Wooden sleeping platform covered with furs

LAB. OF THE NORTH

Canada has several research laboratories in the Arctic. This space age laboratory at Igloolik in Canada's Northwest Territories has contributed much to scientific knowledge of the Arctic region.

Frame for drying skins

Harpoons for hunting seals

Domino-shaped blocks of frozen snow

Last frontiers

RUBBISH DISPOSAL
The way people dispose of their rubbish in the Arctic and Antarctic often pollutes or damages the environment. Rubbish dumps on the edge of Churchill in Canada attract polar bears which can be poisoned or injured by the rubbish. Their proximity also causes fears for people's safety.

Aᴛ ᴛʜᴇ ʜᴇɪɢʜᴛ ᴏꜰ ꜱᴜᴍᴍᴇʀ in the Antarctic, tourist ships move gently around the coast. Even 30 years ago such sights would have been unthinkable, but today people are willing to pay large sums of money to see the last real wilderness in the world. In the Arctic, careless human exploitation in the past has damaged the fragile ecosystem, but today concerned governments are trying to find ways to develop the region while caring for the very special natural environment. Because the Antarctic is less accessible than the Arctic, it is still largely undamaged by humans, although holes in the ozone layer above the Antarctic have already been discovered. Many people believe that one way to preserve the area is to make the whole region into a world park, with any form of exploitation internationally banned. It is important to conserve the Arctic and Antarctic so that future generations can experience these extraordinary environments with their unique wildlife in their natural state.

DAY TRIPPERS
Tourist visits to the Antarctic have to be carefully monitored and organized, as tourists could damage fragile vegetation and disturb nesting and breeding grounds. On the other hand, tourist visits can help to spread concern for conservation.

All snowflakes have six points

LANDS OF SNOW
The permanence of snow and ice in the Arctic and Antarctic regions is what makes them unique. Snow reflects back the sun's rays, helping to keep temperatures low at all times.

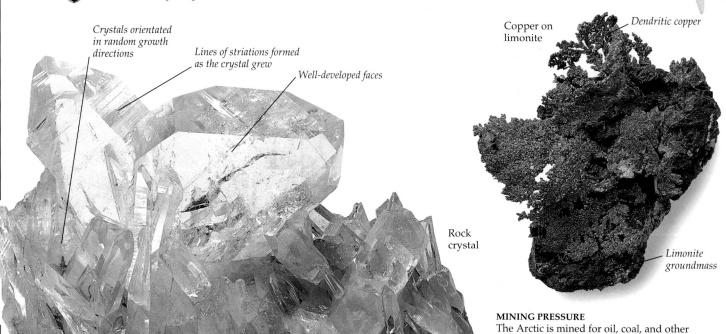

Crystals orientated in random growth directions

Lines of striations formed as the crystal grew

Well-developed faces

Rock crystal

Copper on limonite

Dendritic copper

Limonite groundmass

MINING PRESSURE
The Arctic is mined for oil, coal, and other minerals. Roads, mines, ports, pipelines, and airstrips disturb wildlife and damage the fragile ecosystem. Several minerals have already been found in the Antarctic but the costs of exploiting them, together with increasing pressure to protect the environment, have led the Antarctic Treaty nations to agree to ban mining until 2041.

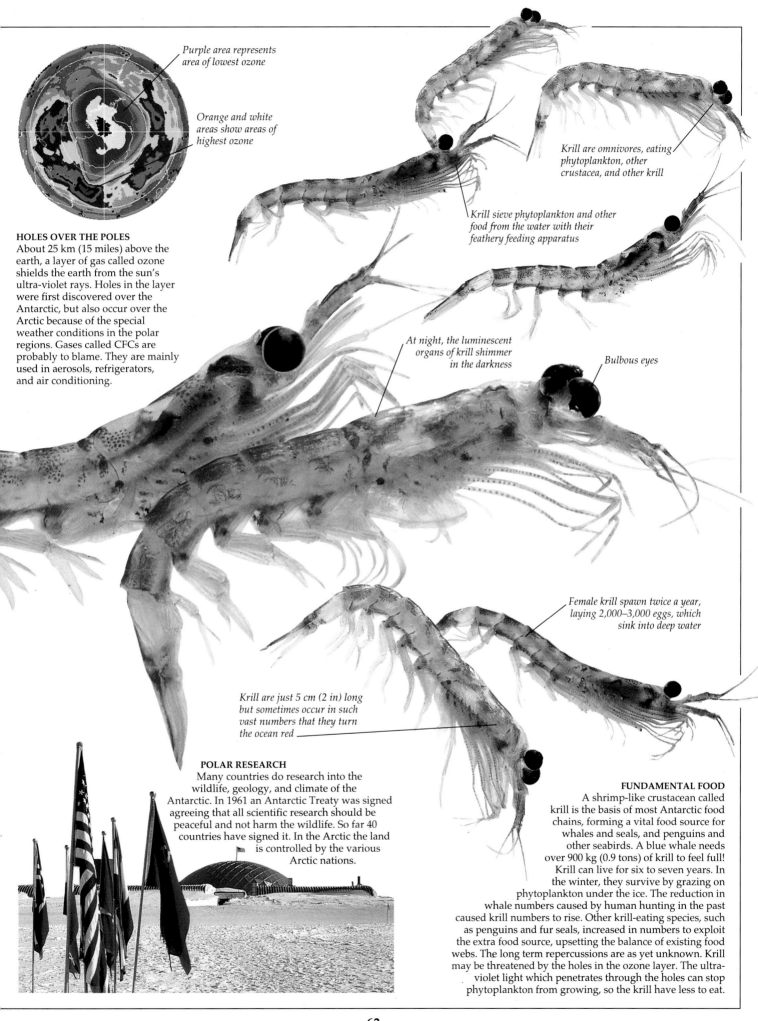

Purple area represents area of lowest ozone

Orange and white areas show areas of highest ozone

HOLES OVER THE POLES

About 25 km (15 miles) above the earth, a layer of gas called ozone shields the earth from the sun's ultra-violet rays. Holes in the layer were first discovered over the Antarctic, but also occur over the Arctic because of the special weather conditions in the polar regions. Gases called CFCs are probably to blame. They are mainly used in aerosols, refrigerators, and air conditioning.

Krill are omnivores, eating phytoplankton, other crustacea, and other krill

Krill sieve phytoplankton and other food from the water with their feathery feeding apparatus

At night, the luminescent organs of krill shimmer in the darkness

Bulbous eyes

Female krill spawn twice a year, laying 2,000–3,000 eggs, which sink into deep water

Krill are just 5 cm (2 in) long but sometimes occur in such vast numbers that they turn the ocean red

POLAR RESEARCH

Many countries do research into the wildlife, geology, and climate of the Antarctic. In 1961 an Antarctic Treaty was signed agreeing that all scientific research should be peaceful and not harm the wildlife. So far 40 countries have signed it. In the Arctic the land is controlled by the various Arctic nations.

FUNDAMENTAL FOOD

A shrimp-like crustacean called krill is the basis of most Antarctic food chains, forming a vital food source for whales and seals, and penguins and other seabirds. A blue whale needs over 900 kg (0.9 tons) of krill to feel full! Krill can live for six to seven years. In the winter, they survive by grazing on phytoplankton under the ice. The reduction in whale numbers caused by human hunting in the past caused krill numbers to rise. Other krill-eating species, such as penguins and fur seals, increased in numbers to exploit the extra food source, upsetting the balance of existing food webs. The long term repercussions are as yet unknown. Krill may be threatened by the holes in the ozone layer. The ultra-violet light which penetrates through the holes can stop phytoplankton from growing, so the krill have less to eat.

Index

Acknowledgments

Dorling Kindersley would like to thank:
Open Air Cambridge Ltd. for the use of their clothing and equipment; the staff of Tierpark Dählhölzli, Bern, Switzerland, for their time and trouble; Tony Hall at the Royal Botanical Gardens, Kew; Julia Nicholson and the Pitt Rivers Museum, Oxford; Robert Headland and the staff of the Scott Polar Institute, Cambridge; Whipsnade Zoo, Bedfordshire; The British School of Falconry, Gleneagles, Scotland; Ivan Finnegan, Kati Poynor, Robin Hunter, Manisha Patel, Andrew Nash, Susan St.Louis, and Aude van Ryn for design and illustration assistance.
Additional photography: Lynton Gardiner at the American Museum of Natural History (60/61b); Neil Fletcher (1c); Dave King (37cr); Minden Pictures (42cl); Harry Taylor at the Natural History Museum (45tl, 47tr); University Museum, Cambridge (43cr); Jerry Young (16cl, 17c, 32/33, 40tl)
Index:
Hilary Bird
Maps:
Sallie Alane Reason
Model:
Gordon Models

Picture credits
t=top b=bottom c=centre l=left r=right

Aardman Animations: 28cr
Ardea: 36c; /Jean-Paul Ferrero 28bc; /François Gohier 45cr; /Graham Robertson 30c
B & C Alexander: 6/7b, 8bl, 11ctr, 15t, 21c, 23c, 25br, 38tl, 39tcr, 42bl, 42/43b, 44bl, 44br, 59c, 60cbl, 61cbr, 62tl, 62tr; /Paul Drummond 23tl; /NASA 63tl
Barnaby's Picture Library /Rothman: 6/7c

Bridgeman Art Library: 25tl; /British Library 7tl; /National Maritime Museum 52cl
British Antarctic Survey: 10tr, 12ctl, 23bl; /D.G. Allan 13 tr, 13br; /C.J. Gilbert 10cl, 10bl, 12tl; /E. Jarvis 45br ; /B. Thomas 61cr
Bruce Coleman Ltd.: 14/15b, 34tl, 35bl, 36bl, 36br; Jen & Des Bartlett 20cl /Roger A. Goggan 12/13; /Johnny Johnson 7tr; /Stephen J. Krasemann 19br; /Len Rue Jr. 40bl; /John Shaw 41c; /Keith Nels Swenson 11ctl; /Rinie van Meurs 29c
ET Archive: 6tr
Mary Evans Picture Library: 8tl, 9tr, 38tr, 40cr, 41tr, 42tl, 46tr, 54bl, 55ct, 55cr, 55bc, 56tl
Illustrated London News: 20tl, 26cr
Frank Lane Picture Agency: /Hannu Hautala 17tcl; /E&D Hosking 22c; /Peter Moore 14cl; /F. Pölking 32cl; /Mark Newman 38c; /Tony Wharton 17tl
Natural History Photographic Agency: /B&C Alexander 10/11; /Melvin Grey 20/21b; /Brian Hawkes 29tl; /Tony Howard /ANT 10c; /E.A. James 29tr;

/Peter Johnson 27c; /Stephen Krasemann 37tr; /Lady Philippa Scott 27bl
Robert Opie Collection: 59cr
Oxford Scientific Films: 27ctl; /Doug Allan 12c, 12b, 16bl, 30tl, 44ctr; /Michael Brooke 22tl; /S.R. Maglione 14/15t; /Colin Monteath 22b; /S.R. Morris 35cl; /Owen Newman 20ctl; /Ben Osborne 26bl, 28l, 29b; /Richard Packwood 36tl; /Konrad Wothe 32bcr
Planet Earth Pictures: /Gary Bell 33tcl; /Peter Scoones 29tc; /Scott McKinley 9cr; /Bora Merdsoy 13bl
Royal Geographical Society: 53cr, 53tr, 56cl; /Alastair Laidlaw 53br
Science Photo Library: /Dr. David Millar 63bl; /Claude Nuridsany & Marie Perennou 62cl
Zefa Picture Library: /Allstock 31c; /Frans Lanting 26tl

Every effort has been made to trace the copyright holders. Dorling Kindersley apologises for any unintentional omissions and would be pleased, in such cases, to add an acknowledgement in future editions.

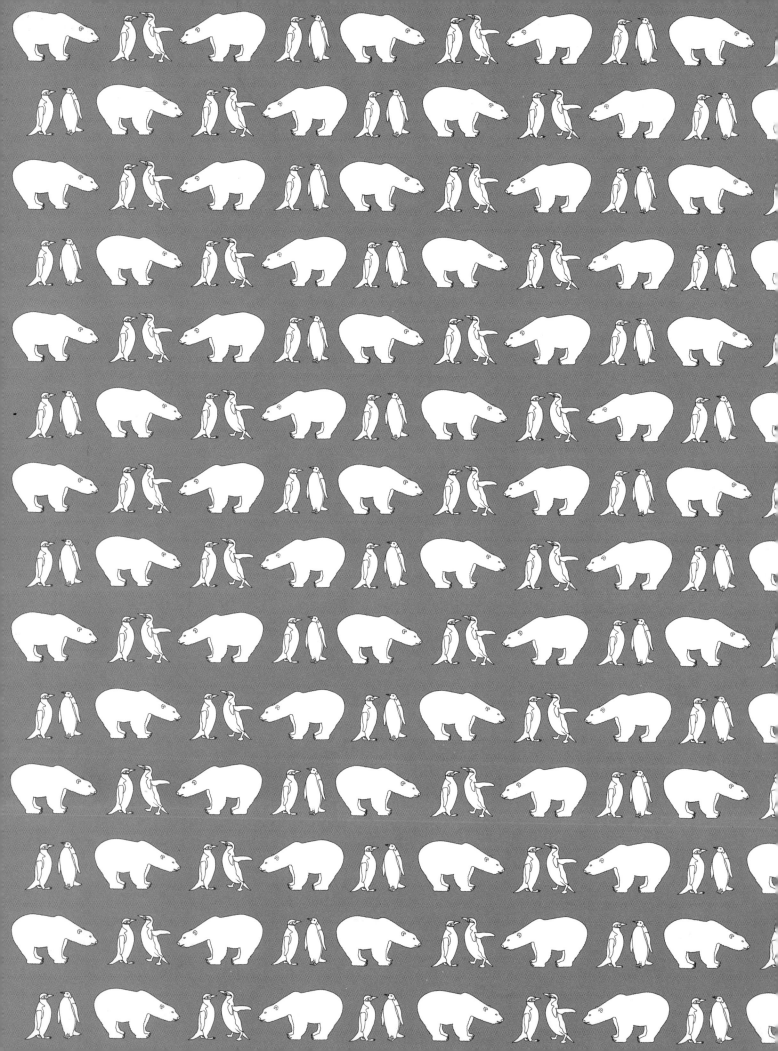